500+ CELEBRITIES:
GO VEGETARIAN
ANIMAL SOULS SERIALIZATION

JACKIE JONES-HUNT PHD

HOUSE OF LIGHT PUBLISHERS LTD

500+ CELEBRITIES: GO VEGETARIAN

Copyright © 2014 Jackie Jones-Hunt
ISBN 978-0-9928661-0-5 PRINT

HOUSE OF LIGHT PUBLISHERS LTD, UK
Author & Owner of House of Light Publishers Ltd:
Jackie Jones-Hunt PhD
First published by
House of Light Publishers Ltd, April 2014

www.jackiejones-hunt.com
Email: jackiejones-hunt@btconnect.com
Tel: 00-44-(0)779-158-8005
Text copyright: Jackie Jones-Hunt PhD 2014

～～～～～～～

The rights of Jackie Jones-Hunt PhD as author have been asserted in accordance with the Copyright, Designs and Patents Act 1988.

A CIP catalogue record for this book is available from the British Library.

House of Light Publishers Ltd seek to utilize an ethical publishing philosophy seeking to disseminate fiction and non-fiction books around the world with an informative, thought-provoking or spiritual message.

WHAT PEOPLE ARE SAYING ABOUT

500+ CELEBRITIES: GO VEGETARIAN

Everybody loves their pets, and many people see their pets on the other side. This research is an important book and I believe it will be popular among NDER's and researchers. Thank you for this excellent contribution to the journey of our soul's literature.

Diane Corcoran PhD.
President of the International Association
for Near Death Studies Inc., USA (IANDS).

Animal Souls is an insightful look into the truth that animals deserve our compassion and respect at the same level as we give to our fellow human animals. Jackie has put to paper so many wonderful descriptions of the complex emotions and interactions we have with all animals. I highly recommend this book and hope it is read far and wide as we could use so much more of the wisdom it contains.

Elizabeth Jane Farians PhD.,
Ohio, USA.
www.veganEarthUS.org

This engrossing serialized volume is a "must read" for all those who consider themselves religiously or spiritually inclined as it stimulates readers to reflect on our true relationship to the rest of sentient creation. I fully and sincerely recommend this outstanding book.

Professor Judith Barad PhD,
Indiana, USA
Author of Aquinas on the Nature and
Treatment of Animals.

It comes as little surprise to me to read in this astonishing, ground-breaking serialized research by Jackie Jones-Hunt PhD that all animals have souls. Every time I look into their eyes I see their souls. They may even have more advanced souls than us.

David Dane
Norfolk, UK,
Landscape Artist
www.dfdaneoilpaintings.co.uk

Pure Gold Again! I am delighted to wholeheartedly endorse Dr. Jackie Jones-Hunt's captivating research. Everyone should read it. It is important to continue to disseminate the 'light' on a global level - to balance the materialistic negative energy one comes across every day. I too, am concerned about animal welfare - the public has to be educated to the horrific animal cruelty which goes on in so many ways...

Victor James Zammit:
Psychical Researcher &
Retired Attorney of the Supreme Court of
New South Wales & the High Court of Australia:
Author of: A Lawyer Presents the Case for the Afterlife,
Irrefutable Objective Evidence.
www.victorzammit.com

I thoroughly endorse and recommend this insightful research split into a series.

Rev. Dr. Elizabeth W. Fenske,
Former: Executive Director of the Spiritual Frontiers
Fellowship International Inc., (SFFI):
Trustee of the Academy of Spirituality & Paranormal Studies Inc:
President of the International Association for Near Death Studies
Inc., (IANDS):
Editor of Vital Signs,
the IANDS Journal,
University Dean & Supervisor for Postgraduate Research, USA.

Two Worlds as a monthly Spiritualist Magazine endorses compassion to animals and so wholeheartedly endorses this well-written serialized research.

There have been a number of credible stories of people on their deathbed seeing their deceased pet companions waiting to greet them. This serialized research suggests an affinity with our pets that transcends physical death. In this intriguing work, Jackie Jones-Hunt PhD helps us incorporate the animal kingdom into our overall spiritual awareness.

This gripping and excellently researched volume split into a series will change lives.

This thought-provoking research awakens us to the fact that many of the founders of religions and spiritual philosophies taught us to show compassion and to commit no harm to our animal relatives. These pages note in view of the modern-day mass slaughter of animals, present-day 'humanity' has lost contact with such spiritual teachings, many of which have become lost, forgotten or distorted. Raising awareness of the authentic, ancient, global spiritual teachings commanding us to show respect and compassion to all animals is enormously important in view of the modern-day plight of animals. Certainly, readers' understanding of Jesus will be profoundly and irrevocably deepened.

"What is religion? Compassion for all things which have life." (Hinduism, Upanishads.) Readers will be unable to put this life-changing series down, alerting us to the fact that all religions command us not to harm animals but to show them compassion. All animals are welcomed and cared for at my ashram in India.

Dr Niranjan Rajyaguru:
Author of 20 books
Spiritual Guru (Teacher) &
Managing Trustee of the Animal Welfare Sanctuary,
Anand Ashram, Gujarat, India.
www.anand-ashram.com/

"Ahimsa-paramo-dharmah" – "Non-injury to living beings is the highest religion (Jainism): Because he has pity on every living creature, therefore is a man called 'holy.'" (Buddhism, Dhammapada). I am pleased to thoroughly recommend this truly inspired life-changing series of books.

Professor Nathalal Gohil:
Author of 25 books on Spiritual Philosophy &
Mysticism, Gujarat, India.

This series of Animal Souls should be read and inwardly digested by all human beings who adhere to the various world religious belief-systems – and who also feel at liberty to still ignore the suffering of animal-kind in their own communities and further afield.

Rev. Lyn Guest de Swarte:
Former Editor of Psychic News,
Hydesville Magazine & Spiritual News:
President of the New Spiritualists' Society:
Internationally renowned teaching medium and healer:
Author of More Principles of Spiritualism.
www.lynguestdeswartepsychicnews.com

Being compassionate to animals should be a fundamental principle from which to order our lives. The Animals Souls series shows us how the most spiritual strands of many of the world's spiritual teachings can bring this about.

Clarissa Baldwin OBE:
Dogs' Trust Chief Executive. Dogs' Trust:
A Dog is For Life
www.dogstrust.org.uk (Registered Charity.)

One Kind welcomes this new serialized book which will help people to re-connect with the other animals with whom we share this planet. They are like us, sentient creatures with thoughts and feelings that matter. What's good for them is ultimately good for us too. After all, humankind, animalkind, we are all One Kind.

Ross Minett:
'One Kind' Science & Research Manager
www.onekind.org (Registered Charity)

We welcome any book that promotes compassion and respect for animals and shows people how to incorporate a philosophy of animal rights into their everyday lives.

Sandra Smiley:
Press Officer PETA, UK.
(People for the Ethical Treatment of Animals)

I endorse books that remind and encourage us to show compassion to animals.

Gordon Smith
International Televised Medium and Author

Dr. Jackie Jones-Hunt's latest excellent and highly informative Animal Souls, series of books, is a "must read." I am Sonia Rinaldi, author of 8 books on Instrumental Transcommunication (ITC): the use of audios/voices and photography and videos proving that life continues after death for all animals, human and non-human.

Presently, in my laboratory, fascinating trans-contacts with dogs are occurring. The photographic and audio experiment results are currently evidencing trans-contacts with dogs proving beyond doubt that dogs (animals) do indeed have post death consciousness and intriguingly, they are able to communicate! The non-human animal communications and photographs received through our apparatus, continues to astonish our dedicated research team.

Prior to these miraculous communications from dogs which also reveal their great sensitivity it was obvious to us that all animals deserve our love and support. After these experiment results - after receiving these on-going after death communications from dogs- myself and my team are emphatic that we should respect all animals even more because these after death communications demonstrate that they have a soul alternatively known as consciousness.

Dr. Jackie Jones-Hunt's fascinating present book is a notable contribution awakening us to the fact that we humans, as their elder brothers and sisters, should demonstrate the utmost compassion and respect to them all!

Sonia Rinaldi,
Brazil: Author of 8 books on ITC:
(Research results clearly & irrefutably demonstrate visual and audible contact & communications with both human and non-human animals after death):
Winner of 3 European Awards for Research.
http://www.ipati.org

As a medium of many years' experience I have received and given proof of the fact that all animals human and non-human survive to the world of spirit. It is refreshing to see that Dr. Jackie Jones-Hunt has written the (serialized) volume Animals Souls clarifying this point and advocating compassion for ALL Animals.

Rev. Gary Cooke
(Minister of Scottish Spiritualist Churches, UK)

As a psychic, psychical researcher with 38 years intense involvement with physical mediumship and its phenomena, I know personally that life continues after physical death for all sentient beings (human and non-human animals). Near death experiencers discuss their life reviews during which they felt the pains of another as if they were their own - these pains were inflicted on others as a result of their neglect or misdeeds during their earlier physical lifetime. Such knowledge should impinge on a person's ever evolving spiritual unfoldment. Consequently, I support this interesting serialized research by Jackie Jones-Hunt PhD which reminds us that we should demonstrate empathy and compassion to all animals during our own lifetimes.

Dr. Robin Foy:
Author of Witnessing the Impossible - the only true & complete report of every sitting of the Scole Experimental Group, 1993-1998.
For Mediumship Advice See:
www.physicalmediumship4u.ning.com

This fascinating research split into a series uncovers long forgotten teachings found in many world religions about humanities relationship with nature. I have run a very busy practice as a Psychic & Medium now for over 10 years, and in all of the thousands of readings I have done, I have been bewildered and often times warmed in my heart to see that animals do in fact survive physical death and carry on in the Afterlife.

The sum of all of my experiences as a 'medium' so far, has led me to the conclusion that life is not defined by physicality. In fact, 'life' is defined by spirit. Whether that be their personality shining through or the brightness of consciousness; I know that my beloved pets are just as "alive" and as real as I am.

I love that Jackie Jones-Hunt PhD has yet again used her research to shine a spotlight on the long forgotten truths that our 'animals' are more than just background scenery in our world - they are our Divine Heritage. And as precious gifts we must cherish them and see to it that they have all of the rights to freedom and peace that we do.

Brough Perkins:
International Televised Medium & Radio Host (USA).
www.broughperkins.ca

Fifteen years ago I lived on a small farm. We rented our land for farmers to fatten their animals and then to be slaughtered. It was then, after seeing my animal friends herded off for the kill I could no longer partake in the eating of those who roam the earth alongside us. As a Medium I have been gifted an insight in the 'lives' of our Animal Kingdom on the 'other side.' Communicating with them on this level has taught me so much about their purpose in the Universe - and it is not to eat them! My faithful companion, Tao, before his death, communicated to me the reason for his coming passing. I cried so much listening to him, on a telepathic level, why it was time for him to leave me. He gave me a completely new understanding to the meaning of 'a dog is a man's/woman's best friend.' He has come to me since his passing often, guiding me, still as my beloved friend-healthy again and happy.

If only we all took some time to understand our animal friends are not just for our food source, or to kill for the thrill of murder, then our very existence on earth wouldbe much richer for remembering who they really are! Allow Dr. Jackie Jones-Hunt's series of books named Animals Souls to enter your heart with a deeper understanding of our non-human beings-it will change your thinking forever!

Jen-Irishu:
Medium & Author of: Messages of Love - My Spiritual Awakening ~ The Angel in My Dreams & The Adventures of Angels & Eli.
www.jen-irishu.com

This timely series of books explores the most spiritually elevated strands of ancient global spiritual teachings (world religions) which teach us to show compassion to animals. I confirm that Spiritualist teachings endorse the most spiritually elevated world religious teachings which implore humankind to show compassion to animals.

Eric Hatton;
Honorary President of the Spiritualists' National Union, Minister of the SNU and Chairman of the JV Trust.

The world badly needs a book about the fact that – like human animals - non-human animals have souls. I admire the courage of Jackie Jones-Hunt PhD in starting the change of paradigm, reversing the damage done to animals through ignorance and arrogance.

Sarah
webmaster for
www.spiritualistresources.com

This fascinating series of books not only raises awareness of the plight of our animals in the world today but also illustrates, through ancient spiritual and religious teachings, that animals have always held a reverend place within cultures throughout the world, throughout time. Sadly, somewhere along the road we have lost sight of the fact that our animals are living sentient beings just like us, capable of feeling love, joy, pain, anxiety and fear. This insightful book beautifully demonstrates that the idea of sharing a world respectfully with love and compassion for all living creatures isn't anything new – but is a belief that is intrinsically embedded within many spiritual and religious traditions.

Sarah-Jane Le Blanc, Author of Pet Whisperer
www.soul2therapy.co.uk

Dr. Jackie Jones-Hunt's understanding of the animal kingdom will make us all sit up and listen the animals need us all to find the truth within our hearts. This series is an essential read. Well done Jackie.

Joanne Hull,
Author of The Pet Psychic & Puppy Tales
www.joannehull.com

This interesting series of books brings a new, well-researched spiritual and religious dimension to animal welfare and environmental matters. I believe it is important to raise awareness of these vital concerns.

Gill Russell,
Anti-Vivisectionist & Animal Welfarist, UK.

This is a very worthwhile serialized volume which should be read in order to understand how important it is to show kindness, mercy and respect to animals and to remind people to be more compassionate to them. The human race seems to have neglected to show compassion to the Animal Kingdom for far too long, but now is the time to rectify this.

Melody Macdonald (Pemberton):
Author of Caught in the Act: (The Feldberg Expose, 1990)
melodypemberton@mac.com

It took me a year to walk from Britain to the Far East to study spiritual philosophy and martial arts for health and protection with the vegetarian Buddhist monks in their shaolin temple who kindly welcomed me. I learned many things including that all animals live in harmony with nature, with the exception of the human animal who has divorced itself from its animal relatives and is speedily destroying our shared home, planet earth, which does not belong to us alone! Spiritual philosophy teaches, when you take you must give back and the only species who takes and gives nothing back is the human animal which will have devastating consequences for all.

Dr. Jackie Jones-Hunt's enthralling, entrancing, highly informed and perceptive research is in harmony with such soul-touching, profoundly elevated compassionate spiritual teachings. I cannot recommend Jackie's extremely vital, insightful and powerful series of animal books more highly. The results of her captivating, fascinating and compelling research will change your life forever.

Mike Gavaghan,
Wildlife Consultancy: Specializing in
All Protected Species & Badgers.

As a dog specialist for various breeds for over 40 years, championship show-breed specialist judge for the world famous Crufts (founded in 1891) and top UK breeder 2008-2011, I am extremely enthusiastic to thoroughly recommend Dr. Jackie Jones-Hunt's "Animal Souls." This research is fascinating and enlightening, raising awareness of the ancient, typically vegetarian, compassionate, spiritual teachings regarding animals which lay at the foundations of world religions. This research reminds all of us human animals to treat all of our fellow, emotional, sentient, feeling, flesh and blood animals with the respect and compassion every one of these individuals rightly deserve.

Gordon Rattray:
Championship Show-Breed Specialist Judge for the world famous
Crufts and Top UK Breeder, 2008-2011.

Fascinating, well-written and inspiring, one of the best books we have read. Having spent our entire lives working with dogs, Parson Russell Terriers in particular, we are pleased to say we thoroughly recommend this fascinating and thought-provoking serialized book.

Jimmy and Louise Scott,
Cambridge, England, UK.

I wholeheartedly recommend this serialized volume to everyone who loves animals.

Steve Hutchins:
The originator & healing breeder of the famous Ratpack Terriers
of the International Breeding & Kennel Club Show Kennels ~
Nurturing Happy, Healthy & Contented Parson Russell Terriers in
mind, body & spirit with 100% Temperament.

FOREWORD

John F. Robins, Secretary to the Charities Animal Concern Advice Line, Save Our Seals Fund & Pressure groups: Animal Concern & Scottish Anti-Vivisection Society.

www.animalconcern.org
www.saveoursealsfund.org
www.adviceaboutanimals.info

As a non-believer I believe that this series will be a vital tool in the crusade to gain protection for animals within the religions of the world. Jackie Jones-Hunt PhD is a believer and has no anti-religious axe to grind. She simply seeks to remind people of faith that in their own teachings they will find good reasons for respecting and protecting animals.

We are in the 21st century of the Christian calendar. Yet in 2011 a Christian church in Scotland refused to lease their hall for a Cruelty-Free Fair as they thought it wrong to promote vegetarianism and animal welfare issues because their version of God had given them "dominion over animals." Other Christian churches continue to exercise their dominion over animals in festivals dedicated to death in village squares, pulling the heads off live geese, putting burning tar balls on the horns of bulls, spearing bulls with lances and blowing thousands of steel-tipped darts at terrified bulls as they run through the streets. Nuns make those steel-tipped darts with the same hands that prepare the Eucharist.

Christianity is not the only religion to indulge in animal sacrifice. Every year hundreds of millions of animals have their throats cut without stunning to meet the requirements of different faiths. On certain holidays around the world animals are killed as offerings to supreme beings. Once every five years in the month of November upwards of a quarter of a million animals are hacked to death in Nepal to honor a Hindu goddess.

If Jackie Jones-Hunt PhD can remind people of faith that their own religions recognize that animals have at least some rights this serialized research will make this planet a better place for the creatures unfortunate enough to have to share it with us.

DEDICATION

This book is dedicated to all 2-legged and 4-legged members of my family, my husband Tony, grandparents Elizabeth-Eileen and Bob, my mother and father Eric and Eileen, and my devoted, mischievous, emotional, intelligent Jack Russell's and Parson Russell Terriers Jac, Sioux, Edward, Lizzie and Eric.

Each of my dogs has taught me so much, including the fact that these flesh and blood, conscious, thinking, feeling, sentient beings, like us, very definitely have souls as a fact of nature.

Jac, Sioux and Edward have passed to spirit and each of them, after their transition to the non-physical realms, has, in very different ways, repeatedly made their presence around me immensely and unquestionably clear.

Sri Aurobindo

Life is life - whether in a cat, or dog or man. There is no difference there between a cat and a man. The idea of difference is a human conception for man's own advantage.

Joseph Addison (1672-1719), English Essayist and Poet

True benevolence or compassion, extends itself through the whole of existence and sympathizes with the distress of every creature capable of sensation.

Akbarati Jetha (Islam)

There can never be peace and happiness in the world so long as we exploit other living creatures for food or otherwise.

A WORD FROM THE AUTHOR

In this installment of my Animal Souls volume, I simply stand back and let my compilation of the following quotations, conveying the most splendid, all-encompassing compassion and the finest wisdom concerning fellow animals speak for themselves.

The reader will see that the same universal sentiment of heart-felt kindness to all animals has been variously articulated by the noblest and most soul-searching individuals from across the globe, since the beginning of time to present day. These men and women from all cultures and all centuries have voiced their heartfelt, astute sentiments. Their bleeding hearts empathize with the murder, suffering, terror, experimentation and callous neglect of innocent, child-like animals, lost, unprotected and incredibly vulnerable in a world dominated by the aggressive human animal and its merciless, cold-blooded, industrialized, killing machines.

Often slowly, piece by piece, these murderous machines cut and slash, draining the life out of traumatized feeling, flesh and blood animals, who, like us, feel and fear suffering and murder. Every few minutes, each and every year, this mechanized homicide slaughters millions of terrified, agonized, flesh and blood, conscious, emotional and thinking innocent infants!

Throughout history these high-minded, like-minds have remained painfully aware, that if the human animal does not show kindness, respect and non-violence to our related animal family, demonstrated through vegetarianism, they will never learn to show these qualities to fellow humans and the human race will never live in peace and harmony.

My research for Animal Souls grew and grew organically, like the roots of a strong and healthy climbing plant, digging deeper and deeper into authentic, undistorted religious historical teachings. I asked for help from the celestial spheres, perhaps this is evidence I received it. Hence my findings are being published in installments, rather than in one large book as previously anticipated. Importantly, each installment can be read independently.

I let the following precious, invaluable, insightful utterances now speak for themselves, revealing the true nature of wisdom, uniting ecological and environmental conservation and all-embracing philanthropy with elevated spirituality.

Joseph Addison (1672-1719), English Essayist and Poet

A man [or woman] must be both stupid and uncharitable who believes there is no virtue or truth but on his own side.

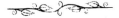

Joseph Addison (1672-1719), English Essayist and Poet

True benevolence or compassion, extends itself through the whole of existence and sympathizes with the distress of every creature capable of sensation.

Rev. R.C.R. Adkins, M.A: Extract from Religion and the Rights of Animals: The British Vegetarian, November/December 1967 (Journal of the Vegetarian Society).

We must act, and act quickly, to see that the rights of animals to a happy life is recognized...A religion, in fact, which fails to recognize these rights cannot be thought of as true religion.

Theodore Adorno

Auschwitz happens when people look at a slaughterhouse and think they are only animals.

Aesop (c. 620-564 BCE), Ancient Greek Writer: Acclaimed as the author of many internationally famous animal fables still celebrated today.

Beware lest you lose the substance by grasping at the shadow.

Aesop (c. 620-564 BCE), Ancient Greek Writer: Acclaimed as the author of many internationally famous animal fables still celebrated today.

It is easy to be brave from a safe distance.

Aesop (c. 620-564 BCE), Ancient Greek Writer: Acclaimed as the author of many internationally famous animal fables still celebrated today.

No act of kindness, no matter how small, is ever wasted.

Aesop (c. 620-564 BCE), Ancient Greek Writer: Acclaimed as the author of many internationally famous animal fables still celebrated today.

We hang the petty thieves and appoint the great ones to public office.

Akbarati Jetha: Teacher of Islam

There can never be peace and happiness in the world so long as we exploit other living creatures for food or otherwise.

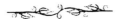

Bob Allen

Remember, no one has ever built strong, trusting, respectful, harmonious or peaceful relationships with anyone, human or animal...by using intimidation, fear, force, or pain...they never have, and they never will...

Frederick (Henri Frederic) Amiel, (1821-1881), Swiss Philosopher and Poet

Truth is not only violated by falsehood; it may be equally outraged by silence.

Frederick (Henri Frederic) Amiel, (1821-1881), Swiss Philosopher and Poet

Truth is the secret of eloquence and of virtue, the basis of moral authority. It is the highest summit of art and life.

Frederick (Henri Frederic) Amiel, (1821-1881), Swiss Philosopher and Poet

Truth above all, even when it upsets us and overwhelms us.

Georg Thorndike Angell (1823-1909), American Lawyer, Philanthropist and Advocate for the humane treatment of animals.

I am sometimes asked, 'Why do you spend so much of your time and money talking about kindness to the animals when there is so much cruelty to men?' I answer, 'I am working at the roots.'

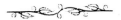

Frederick (Henri Frederic) Amiel, (1821-1881), Swiss Philosopher and Poet

if man was what he ought to be, he would be adored by the animals...

Aristotle (384-322 B.C.) Greek Philosopher, Scientist, Logician (Student of Plato)

The high-minded man [person] must take care more for truth than for what people think.

Cleveland Amory (1917-1998), Harvard Crimson Editor, TV Guide and Parade Columnist

I consider the three most cruelly produced foods to be from lobsters, dropped alive into boiling water, veal from calves separated from their mothers and kept in crates, and pate de fois gras. (Pate de foie gras is covered in the film Mondo Kane which shows the force feeding of geese. Food is stuffed down their throats with a pole....when they want to regurgitate...a brass ring is tied around their throat...the excess food creates a stuffed liver pleasing to gourmets). (Caviar comes from the ripping out of the ovaries of the mother sturgeon fish).

4

American Proverb

You are what you eat.

Dr. Thomas Arnold (1795-1842), Historic Headmaster of the famous Rugby School, UK

It would seem as if the primitive Christian, by laying so much stress upon a future life in contradistinction to this life, and placing the lower creatures out of the pale of hope, placed them at the same time out of the pale of sympathy, and thus laid the foundation for this utter disregard of animals in the light of our fellow creatures...

Bea Arthur

Many years ago, I was in a Broadway show and I had to wear a fox fur around my shoulders. One day my hand touched one of the fox's legs. It seemed to be in two pieces. Then it dawned on me.... her leg had probably been snapped in two by the steel trap that had caught it.

Meher Baba (1894-1969)

If we understand and feel that the greatest act of devotion and worship to God is not to harm any of His beings, we are loving God.

Meher Baba (1894-1969)

To love God in the most practical way is to love our fellow beings. If we feel for others in the same way as we feel for our own dear ones, we love God.

Meher Baba (1894-1969)

If we suffer in the sufferings of others and feel happy in the happiness of others, we are loving God.

Sir Frances Bacon (1561-1626), English Author, Courtier, and Philosopher

The more noble a soul is, the more objects of compassion it has.

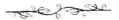

Sir Frances Bacon (1561-1626), English Author, Courtier, and Philosopher

Praise from the common people is generally false, and rather follows the vain than the virtuous.

The Rt. Revd. Dr. John Austin Baker: Extract from a published letter in the Church of England Newspaper, 25th September 2003

'Human rights' is a complex idea and one may agree that animal and human 'rights' are not precisely on a par. If, however, humans have 'an obligation to see that animals do not suffer ... pain', then it is an animal's 'right' that we should honor that obligation.

Matt Ball, Vegan Outreach Co-founder

We are the lucky ones - we are not standing day after day in a tiny space, breathing the stench of our own waste, waiting only to be slaughtered. We must do everything possible for those suffering lives of pain and terror.

Neal Barnard

The beef industry has contributed to more American deaths than all the wars of this century, all natural disasters, and all automobile accidents combined. If beef is your idea of "real food for real people" you'd better live real close to a real good hospital.

The Revd. Professor William Barclay: Extract from Man and the Beasts - Life and Work: Church of Scotland Magazine, January 1976

The rights of animals are protected [in religious teachings]. The animals must have their day of rest as men must have it (Exodus 20.10; 23.12). If a nest is harried, the mother bird must never be killed, but must always be let go (Deuteronomy 22. 6, 7). When the ox is drawing the heavy sled that threshes the grain, he must never be muzzled. He must, as it were, be allowed to have a share in the fruit of his labors (Deuteronomy 25.4).

Drew Barrymore, American Actress

The thing that has been weighing on my mind this week is that I wanted to go and save all the little live lobsters in restaurants and throw them back in the ocean. Imagine me being arrested for that? Honest chefs will confirm that lobsters like other shell fish, SCREAM when immersed in boiling water to be boiled alive. [They feel pain as they have nervous systems].

Christian Barnard M.D. Heart Surgeon

I had bought two male chimps from a primate colony in Holland. They lived next to each other in separate cages for several months before I used one as a [non-volunteer heart] donor. When we put him to sleep in his cage in preparation for the operation, he chattered and cried incessantly. We attached no significance to this, but it must have made a great impression on his companion, for when we removed the body to the operating room, the other chimp wept bitterly and was inconsolable for days. The incident made a deep impression on me. I vowed never again to experiment with such sensitive creatures.

O.A. Battista

A dog is one of the remaining reasons why some people can be persuaded to go for a walk.

Henry Ward Beecher (1813-1887)

For fidelity, devotion, love, many a two-legged animal is below the dog and the horse. Happy would it be for thousands of people if they could stand at last before the Judgment Seat and say 'I have loved as truly and I have lived as decently as my dog.' And yet we call them 'only brutes'!

Nicholas Berdyaev (1874-1948), Russian Religious and Political Philosopher: Dostoievsky (sic) An Interpretation, Translated by Donald Attwater (New York: Sheed and Ward, 1934), P204

The will-to-power deprives of freedom both those who wield and those who are subject to it, and Christ knew no power except that of love, which alone is compatible with freedom. His is the religion of unconstrained love between God and man, and the attempts to actualize this in Christianity have generally been very far indeed from our Lord's own conception.

Henry Beston (1888-1968), Author

For the animal shall not be measured by man. In a world older and more complete than ours, they move finished and complete, gifted with extensions of the senses we have lost or never attained, living by voices we shall never hear. They are not brethren; they are not underlings; they are other nations, caught with ourselves in the net of life and time, fellow prisoners of the splendor and travail of the Earth.

Henry Ward Beecher (1813-1887)

The dog was created especially for children. He is the god of frolic.

Jeremy Bentham (1748-1832), This excellent scholar began his degree at Oxford University, UK, at the age of 12, later becoming a Utilitarian Philosopher, Social Reformer, Economist and Jurist. Extract from the: Introduction to the Principles of Morals and Legislation

Other animals, which, on account of their interests having been neglected by the insensibility of the ancient jurists, stand degraded into the class of 'things.'...The day has been, I grieve it to say, in many places it is not yet past, in which the greater part of the species, under the denomination of slaves, have been treated...upon the same footing as...animals are still. The day may come, when the rest of the animal creation may acquire those rights which never could have been witholden from them but by the hand of tyranny. The French have already discovered that the blackness of skin is no reason why a human being should be abandoned to the caprice of a tormentor. It may come one day to be recognized, that the number of legs, the villosity of the skin, or the termination of the os sacrum, are reasons equally insufficient for abandoning a sensitive being to the same fate.
What else is it that should trace the insuperable line? Is it the faculty of reason or perhaps the faculty of discourse? But a full-grown horse or dog is beyond comparison a more rational, as well as more conversable animal, than an infant of a day or a week or even a month old. But suppose they were otherwise, what would it avail? The question is not, Can they reason? Nor can they talk? But: Can they suffer? Why should the law refuse its protection to any sensitive being?... The time will come when humanity will extend its mantle over everything which breathes...

Nicholas Berdyaev (1874-1948), Russian Religious and Political Philosopher

There are plenty of dead things in Christianity, and their putrefaction spreads pestilence that can poison the well-springs of life. In some respects Christians are more like minerals than parts of a living organism: we are petrified, dead words come out from our lifeless mouths. 'The Spirit breatheth where he will' and he will not breathe upon souls that are religiously desiccated: they must be first remade and baptized anew, but with fire. Progress of the antichristian spirit, loss of faith, spread of materialism these are only secondary results, the consequences of the stiffening and death that has gone on within Christianity, in the lives of Christians. A Christianity given over to stereotyped rhetoric, formal and spiritless in its rites, debased by clericalism or laicizing cannot be a life-giving force. Yet it is from Christianity that regeneration and renewal of the spirit must come; if it is truly the timeless and eternal religion, then it has to be the religion of the new age that is upon us, and there must arise within her a creative movement as the world has not known for a long time.

Rynn Berry, Author, Educator and Speaker

My perspective of veganism was most affected by learning that the veal calf is a by-product of dairying, and that in essence there is a slice of veal in every glass of what I had thought was an innocuous white liquid - MILK.

Ambrose Gwinnett Bierce (1842-1913) American Editorialist, Journalist, Short-story Writer and Satirist, famed for his Devil's Dictionary: Extract below

'Fork:' An instrument used chiefly for the purpose of putting dead animals into the mouth.

11

Besant (1847-1933), the English Philosopher, Humanitarian and Social Reformer who worked for Indian independence.

> [Individuals who eat animal flesh] are responsible for all the pain that grows out of meat-eating, and which is necessitated by the use of sentient animals as food; not only the horrors of the slaughterhouse, but also the preliminary horrors of the railway traffic, of the steamboat and ship traffic; all the starvation and the thirst and the prolonged misery of fear which these unhappy creatures have to pass through for the gratification of the appetite of man...All pain acts as a record against humanity and slackens and retards the whole of human growth...

Guy Berkeley 'Berke' American Cartoonist, Bloom County, Babylon, USA

> Dear Lord, I've been asked, nay commanded, to thank Thee for the Christmas turkey before us... a turkey which was no doubt a lively, intelligent bird... a social being...capable of actual affection... nuzzling its young with almost human-like compassion. Anyway, it's dead and we're gonna eat it. Please give our respects to its family.

Elizabeth Blackwell M.D. First American woman to gain a medical degree in the USA (1849); graduating first in her class. Emily, her sister was the second.

> The excuse or toleration of cruelty upon any living creature by a woman is a deadly sin against the grandest force in nature – maternal love. In not a single instance known to science has the cure of any human disease resulted necessarily from this fallacious method of research.

Henry Beston (1888-1968), Author: Extract from: The Outermost House

We need another and a wiser and perhaps a more mystical concept of animals. Remote from universal nature and living by complicated artifice, man in civilization surveys the creature through the glass of his knowledge and sees thereby a feather magnified and the whole image in distortion. We patronize them for their incompleteness, for their tragic fate for having taken form so far below ourselves. And therein do we err. For the animal shall not be measured by man. In a world older and more complete than ours, they move finished and complete, gifted with the extension of the senses we have lost or never attained, living by voices we shall never hear. They are not brethren, they are not underlings: they are other nations, caught with ourselves in the net of life and time, fellow prisoners of the splendor and travail of the earth.

Ambrose Gwinnett Bierce (1842-1913) American Editorialist, Journalist, Short-story Writer and Satirist, famed for his Devil's Dictionary

The most affectionate creature in the world is a wet dog.

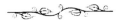

Henry J. Bigelow, M.D: Extract from Animal Times, Winter 2003

There will come a time when the world will look back to modern vivisection in the name of Science, as they do now to burning at the stake in the name of religion.

William Blake (1757-1827), English Poet

Where mercy, love, and pity dwell, there God is dwelling too.

Lloyd Biggle Jr.

Life is life's greatest gift. Guard the life of another creature as you would your own because it is your own. On life's scale of values, the smallest is no less precious to the creature who owns it, than the largest.

Wilfrid Scawen Blunt (1840-1922)

The atrocious doctrine that beast and birds were made solely for man's use and pleasure, and that he has no duties towards them.

Steve Bluestone

Did you ever notice when you blow in a dog's face he gets mad at you? But when you take him in a car he sticks his head out the window.

Dietrich Bonheoffer (1906-1945), Christian German Lutheran Pastor and Theologian

Silence in the case of evil [when aware of evil] is itself evil.

Dietrich Bonhoeffer (1906-1945) Christian German Lutheran Pastor and Theologian: Extract from: The Cost of Discipleship (New York: McMillan, 1963), P188.

If there is no element of asceticism in our lives, if we give free rein to the desires of the flesh...we shall find it hard to train for the service of Christ.

William Booth (General) (1829-1912), Founder of the Salvation Army

> It is a great delusion to suppose that flesh of any kind is essential to health.

Robert Brault, Writer

> For the most part, we carnivores do not eat other carnivores. We prefer to eat our vegetarian friends.

Allen Brantley, FBI Supervisory Special Agent

> Animal cruelty...is not a harmless venting of emotion in a healthy individual; this is a warning sign that this individual is not mentally healthy and needs some sort of intervention. Abusing animals does not dissipate these violent emotions, it may fuel them.

Robert Brault, Freelance Writer

> An old dog, even more than an old spouse, always feels like doing what you feel like doing.

David Brenner

> A vegetarian is a person who won't eat anything that can have children.

Brennan Browne, Animal Rights Activist

Man IS superior to every other being in his ability to excuse away those parts of himself too vile for self-examination.

Brigit Brophy (1929-1995), British Novelist, Campaigner for Social Reforms and the Rights of Animals

I don't hold animals superior or even equal to humans. The whole case for behaving decently to animals rests on the fact that we are the superior species. We are the species uniquely capable of imagination, rationality, and moral choice - and that is precisely why we are under an obligation to recognize and respect the rights of animals.

Rev. O. A. Broadley: A Vegetarian Church: Extract from: An Address delivered at the Bible Christian Church, Cross Lane, Salford, on October 14th 1906 :Extract from a transcript in The Vegetarian Messenger and Health Review: November 1906

The day is coming when the dogma which binds the churches in fetters will be dispensed with and the spirit of true brotherhood will take its place. As the world realizes more fully the Divine sonship of the race, that all life is one, and that God is the Father of all, there will come also the realization of its responsibility. With the realization of kinship with all creatures, including those in the lower order of creation, there will come a sense of duty to them and that we must show our nobility by exercising our right of merciful justice, and not by our power to oppress the poor merciful beasts.

Brennan Browne, Animal Rights Activist

Animal Rights - Rational, not Radical.

Brennan Browne, Animal Rights Activist

Humanely 'slaughtered 'meat,' is an obscene lie invented and perpetuated by people who are too lazy, selfish and cruel to change their dietary habits. Forcibly denying a creature its right to life, love and companionship can NEVER be humane.

Brigit Brophy (1929-1995), British Novelist, Campaigner for Social Reforms and the Rights of Animals

Whenever people say, 'We mustn't be sentimental,' you can take it that they are about to do something cruel. And if they add, 'We must be realistic,' they mean they are going to make money from it.

Jeffrey Brown

Why would it be necessary for human beings to drink the milk of another mammal to be healthy? A mother cow's milk is designed specifically for her calf; likewise, a human mother's milk is designed specifically for a human baby. Does the calf have to drink the human mother's milk to be healthy? If not, then why should a human being drink the milk of a cow to be healthy?

Robert Browning

God made all the creatures and gave them our love and our fear, to give sign; we and they are His children, one family here.

Brennan Browne, Animal Rights Activist

The concept of 'animal rights' values the simple premise that ALL living creatures have a 'right' to be allowed to live their lives without victimization - free from brutality. It is a right that EVERY being strives for.

Brennan Browne, Animal Rights Activist

Compassion counts above all else - more than intelligence, wealth, power or prominence. Those who have it, and extend it to ALL living beings, fully understand its potential to single-handedly change the world.

Elijah D. Buckner MD, AM, PhD (1843-1907)

It is a deplorable fact that many Christians are so accustomed to a certain creed and dogma of their own that they will adhere to it even at the sacrifice of the great moral laws of love and mercy.

Brennan Browne, Animal Rights Activist

You are now entering the Twilight Zone. A place where benevolence toward all life forms is TERRORISM punishable by prison today...likely, death tomorrow. Savage, unbridled slaughter is the norm, defended as just and humane, as long as money and power remain the blood-soaked, unholy grail. That's the signpost up ahead. Next stop. A place where lies are proselytized as truth; stupidity as wisdom; torture and death as honorable tradition, and contempt, arrogance and rape, as benign and sustainable. The 'human hood' - presently lost, insane and rabid within its own cage - planet Earth.

Pearl S. Buck (1892-1973), American Author

You cannot make yourself feel something you don't feel. But you can make yourself do right, in spite of your feelings.

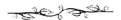

Elijah D. Buckner MD., AM., PhD. (1843-1907)

Man should regard lower animals as being in the same dependent condition as minors under his government ... For a man to torture an animal whose life God has put into his hands, is a disgrace to his species.

Elijah D. Buckner MD, AM, PhD (1843-1907) ~ Extract from The Immortality of Animals

...The Bible, without the shadow of a doubt, recognizes that animals have living souls the same as man. Most of the quotations given are represented as having been spoken by the Creator Himself, and he certainly knows whether or not He gave to man and lower animals alike a living soul, which of course means an immortal soul.

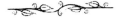

Buddha (563-483 BC)

May all that have life be delivered from suffering.

Buddha (563-483 BC)

When a man has pity on all living creatures then only is he noble.

Buddha (563-483 BC)

All beings tremble before violence, all fear death, all love life, see yourself in others, and then whom can you hurt? What harm can you do?

Buddha (563-483 BC): Extract from the Lankavatara Sutra

For fear of causing terror to living beings...let the Bodhisattva who is disciplining himself to attain compassion refrain from eating flesh.

Buddhism, Dhammapada

Because he has pity on every living creature, therefore is a man called holy.

Buddha (563-483 BC): Extract from the Lankavatara Sutra
For the sake of love of purity, the Bodhisattva should refrain from eating flesh, which is born of semen, blood, etc., for fear of causing terror to living beings let the Bodhisattva, who is disciplining himself to attain compassion, refrain from eating flesh...It is not true that meat is proper food and permissible when the animal was not killed by himself, when he did not order others to kill it, when it was not specially meant for him. Again, there may be some people in the future who...being under the influence of the taste for meat will string together in various ways sophisticated arguments to defend meat eating. But...meat eating in any form, in any manner and in any place is unconditionally and once and for all prohibited...Meat eating I have not permitted to anyone, I do not permit, I will not permit.

The Buddhist Mahaparinirvana

The eating of meat extinguishes the seed of great compassion.

Edmund Burke (1729-1797), Irish born English Statesman, Orator and Writer

All that is needed for the triumph of evil is that good men do nothing.

Robert Burns (1759-1796), Scottish Poet: Extract From: On scaring some Waterfowl

But man to whom alone is given,
A ray direct from pitying Heaven,
Glories in his heart humane,
And creatures for his pleasure slain.

Isaac Bustos, age 9, Public School 32, Bronx, New York, USA

I think that people should start eating less meat. In case you haven't noticed, meat is made out of animals. How would you feel if you were a baby pig separated from your mother and about to be turned into bacon? We don't eat dogs and cats because they are cute. Well, pigs can be just as cute if you give them a chance.

Samuel Butler: Note-Books, 1912

Man is the only animal that can remain on friendly terms with the victims he intends to eat until he eats them.

Samuel Butler: Note-Books, 1912

The great pleasure of a dog is that you may make a fool of yourself with him and not only will he not scold you, but he will make a fool of himself too.

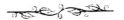

Karel Čapek

> If dogs could talk, perhaps we would find it as hard to get along with them as we do with people.

Brennan T. Casey

> Poor animals! How jealously they guard their pathetic bodies . . . that which to us is merely an evening's meal, but to them is life itself.

C. Richard Calore: The Rights of Animals: Voice of the Voiceless

> Many times I'm told I should stop protecting animals and start protecting people. I'm deeply concerned about the poor/the children/the elderly/the sick and those persecuted because of race, color and creed. Their suffering is my suffering, but at least they can talk for their own defense; animals cannot!

T. Colin Campbell PhD., Professor of Nutrition, Cornell University, USA

In the next ten years, one of the things you're bound to hear is that animal protein is one of the most toxic nutrients of all that can be considered.

Roger Caras

Dogs are not our whole life, but they make our lives whole.

T. Colin Campbell PhD., Professor of Nutrition, Cornell University, USA (Letter Dated 3/29/98)

In every respect, vegans appear to enjoy equal or better health in comparison to both vegetarians and non-vegetarians.

T. Colin Campbell PhD., Professor of Nutrition, Cornell University, USA

Quite simply, the more you substitute plant foods for animal foods, the healthier you are likely to be. I now consider veganism to be the ideal diet. A vegan diet – particularly one that is low in fat – will substantially reduce disease risks. Plus, we've seen no disadvantages from veganism.

Bliss Carman (William Bliss Carman) (1861-1929), Canadian Poet

The greatest joy in nature is the absence of man.

T. Colin Campbell PhD., Professor of Nutrition, Cornell University, USA

> Usually, the first thing a country does in the course of economic development is to introduce a lot of livestock. Our data are showing that this is not a very smart move.... We are basically a vegetarian species and should be eating a wide variety of plant food and minimizing our intake of animal foods.... Once people start introducing animal products into their diet, that's when the mischief starts.

Louis J. Camuti (1893-1981), Veterinarian and Author of: All My Patients are Under the Bed: Memoirs of a Cat Doctor

> Never believe that animals suffer less than humans. Pain is the same for them as it is for us. Even worse, because they cannot help themselves.

Louis J. Camuti (1893-1981), Veterinarian and Author of: All My Patients are Under the Bed: Memoirs of a Cat Doctor

> Love of animals is a universal impulse, a common ground on which all of us may meet. By loving and understanding animals, perhaps we humans shall come to understand each other.

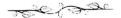

Thomas Carlyle (1795-1881), A Scotsman and English Historian, Biographer and Essayist

> What is philosophy but a continual battle, an ever-renewed effort to transcend the sphere of blind custom and so become transcendental.

Roger Caras

Dogs have given us their absolute all. We are the center of their universe. We are the focus of their love and faith and trust. They serve us in return for scraps. It is without a doubt the best deal man has ever made.

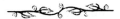

Bliss Carman (William Bliss Carman) (1861-1929), Canadian Poet
There is only one way in the world to be distinguished: Follow your instinct! Be yourself, and you'll be somebody. Be one more blind follower of the blind and you will have the oblivion you desire.

Judy Carman, Author: Extract from Peace to All Beings, Veggie Soup for the Chicken's Soul, (P41)

I am thinking of the many, who are still holding their sense of mercy in check for fear of social disapproval. I kept mine in check for too long. And each time I let it out, I felt the pressure to conform – true enough. What helped me? It was seeing others speak out, be ridiculed and have the courage and inner certainty to speak out again and again. If we can be desensitized to animals' pain, then we can also desensitize ourselves to being ridiculed and pressured.

Bliss Carman (William Bliss Carman) (1861-1929), Canadian Poet

Set me a task into which I can put something of my very self, and it is a task no longer. It is joy and art.

Bliss Carman (William Bliss Carman) (1861-1929), Canadian Poet

What are facts but compromises? A fact merely marks the point where we have agreed to let investigation cease.

Bliss Carman (William Bliss Carman) (1861-1929), Canadian Poet

Whether it be to failure or success, the first need of being is endurance – to endure with gladness if we can, with fortitude in any event.

Rachel Carson (1907-1964), Author of Silent Spring, Biologist and Ecologist

We cannot have peace among men whose hearts
find delight in killing any living creature.

Archdeacon Edward Carpenter, PhD, (He became the Dean of Westminster Abbey): Extract from: Man's Relationship with the Animal Creation – (A Sermon delivered at the Abbey after the publication of the 'Brambell Report' on factory farming.) Transcript published in The British Vegetarian, July-August 1966

It is indeed within the consciousness of a solemn trust, held under the sovereignty of the Most High God the Creator, that man is required to look around at other orders of creation, all of which exist, by divine decree, alongside of him. These orders have their rights, difficult though it may be to define precisely what they are. It is, of course, because of this difficulty that it is easier to talk in general terms; to recognize an over-all responsibility; to see our stewardship as a trust held under God – it is easier to do this rather than to see in practice what this means.

Rachel Carson (1907-1964), Author of Silent Spring, Biologist and Ecologist

Until we have the courage to recognize cruelty for what it is – whether its victim is human or animal – we cannot expect things to be much better in this world...We cannot have peace among men whose hearts delight in killing any living creature. By every act that glorifies or even tolerates such moronic delight in killing we set back the progress of humanity.

Rachel Carson (1907-1964), Author of Silent Spring, Biologist and Ecologist

The more I learned about the use of pesticides, the more appalled I became. I realized that here was the material for a book. What I discovered was that everything which meant most to me as a naturalist was being threatened, and that nothing I could do would be more important.

The Catholic Catechism 2416

Animals are God's creatures. He surrounds them with his providential care. By their mere existence they bless him and give him glory. Thus men owe them kindness. We should recall the gentleness with which saints like St. Francis of Assisi or St. Phillip Neri treated animals.

Holly Cheever, DVM Animal Activist

We should give all animals the benefit of the doubt that they are fully sentient, even   if our senses are too dull to appreciate fully their intelligence.

Cesar Chavez

Kindness and compassion toward all living things is the mark of a civilized society. Conversely, cruelty, whether it is directed against human beings or against animals, is not the exclusive province of any one culture or community of people ... Only when we have become non-violent towards all life will we have learned to live well ourselves.

Judy Chicago (Born Judy Cohen on 20/7/1939), Feminist Artist, Author and Educator: From Eternal Treblinka (P49)

I began to wonder about the ethical distinction between processing pigs and doing the same thing to people defined as pigs. Many would argue that moral considerations do not have to be extended to animals, but this is just what the Nazis said about the Jews.

Chinese Proverb

If you are patient in one moment of anger, you will escape a hundred days of sorrow.

Chief Seattle (1786-1866)

If all the beasts were gone, men would die from a great loneliness of spirit, for whatever happens to the beasts also happens to the man. All things are connected.

Judy Chicago (Born on July 20, 1939 as Judy Cohen), Feminist, Artist, Author and Educator: Extract from Eternal Treblinka, (P50)

I saw the whole globe symbolized at Auschwitz, and it was covered with blood: people being manipulated and used; animals being tortured in useless experiments;   men   hunting helpless, vulnerable creatures for the "thrill"; human beings ground   down by inadequate housing and medical care and by not having enough to eat; men   abusing women and children; people polluting the earth, filling it with poisons that   foul the air, the soil, and the water; the imprisonment of dissident voices; the elimination of people of opposing political views; the oppression of those who look, Feel, or act differently.

An Ancient Chinese Verse

For hundreds of thousands of years
The stew in the pot
Has brewed hatred and resentment
That is difficult to stop.
If you wish to know why there are disasters
Of armies and weapons in the world,
Listen to the piteous cries
From the slaughterhouse at midnight.

Chief Seattle (1786-1866)

This much we know.
The earth does not belong to man;
Man belongs to the earth.This we know.
All things are connected like the blood which unites one family.
All things are connected.
Whatever befalls the earth befalls the sons of the earth.
Man did not weave the web of life; he is merely a strand in it.
Whatever he does to the web, he does to himself.

Chitrabhanuji

Let us pray that our food should not be colored with animal blood and human suffering.

Chief Seattle (1786-1866)

...the deer, the horse, the great eagle, these are our brothers. The rocky crests, the juices in the meadows, the body heat of the pony and man - all belong to the same family... The White Man must treat the beasts of this land as his brothers.

John Chrysostom (A.D. 347-407)

Surely we ought to show kindness and gentleness to animals for many reasons and chiefly because they are of the same origin as ourselves.

John Chrysostom (A.D. 347-407): Extract from the Homilies (Ancient Religious Texts)

The Saints are exceedingly loving and gentle to mankind, and even to brute beasts ... surely we ought to show them (animals) great kindness and gentleness for many   reasons, but, above all, because they are of the same origin as ourselves.

John Chrysostom (A.D. 347-407)

...flesh-meats and wine serve as materials for sensuality, and are a source of danger, sorrow, and disease.

John Chrysostom (A.D. 347-407), A group of exemplary Christians: Homilies 69 (Ancient Religious Texts)

No streams of blood flowed at their place; no flesh was slaughtered and cut to pieces ... One does not smell there the awful vapor of meals of meat ... one hears no racket and terrible noise. They eat only bread, which they earn through their work, and water that a pure spring offers them. When they want a lavish meal, then indulgence consists of fruits, and they find thereby higher enjoyment than at the royal tables.

John Chrysostom (A.D. 347-407)

Holy people are most loving and gentle in their dealings with their fellows, and even with the lower animals: for this reason it was said that 'A righteous man is merciful to the life of his beast...' (Proverbs 12:10)

John Chrysostom (A.D. 347-407)

We imitate the ways of wolves, the ways of leopards; or rather we are worse than these. For nature has assigned that they should be thus fed, but us God hath honored with speech and a sense of equity, yet we are worse than the wild beasts.

John Chrysostom (A.D. 347-407)

We the Christian leaders practice abstinence from the flesh of animals to subdue our bodies...the unnatural eating of flesh-meat is of demonical origin...the eating of flesh is polluting.

Barbara Clayton, DVM Pine Plains, New York, USA: The Register Herald 26 June 2001

I'm a vegetarian and sort of a conscientious objector. I object to eating my patients, so for this reason I don't like to treat animals that are raised for food.

C. David Coates, Author: Preface from Old MacDonald's Factory Farm

Isn't man an amazing animal? He kills wildlife by the millions in order to protect his domestic animals and their feed. Then he kills domestic animals by the billions and eats them.
This in turn kills man by the millions, because eating all those animals leads to degenerative - and fatal - health conditions like heart disease, kidney disease, and cancer. So, then man tortures and kills millions more animals to look for cures for these diseases.

Elsewhere, millions of other human beings are being killed by hunger and malnutrition because food they could eat is being used to fatten domestic animals.

[For slaughter]. Meanwhile, some people are dying of sad laughter at the absurdity of man, who kills so easily and so violently and once a year sends out cards praying for 'Peace on Earth.'

Dr. Donald Coggan, Archbishop of Canterbury

Animals, as part of God's creation, have rights which must be respected. It behoves us always to be sensitive to their needs and to the reality of their pain.

The Code of Jewish Law, Sephardic Compilation of Jewish Law 1560

It is forbidden according to the Torah, to inflict pain upon any living creature. On the contrary, it is our duty to relieve the pain of any creature, even if it is ownerless or belongs to a non-Jew.

J. M. Coetzee: From Eternal Treblinka (P51)

Let me say it openly: we are surrounded by an enterprise of degradation, cruelty, and killing which rivals anything the Third Reich was capable of, indeed dwarfs it, in that ours is an enterprise without end, self-regenerating, bringing rabbits, rats, poultry, livestock ceaselessly into the world for the purpose of killing them.

Samuel Taylor Coleridge (1772-1834) English Poet: The Rime of the Ancient Mariner: Part VII

Both man and bird and beast.
He prayeth best, who loveth best
All things both great and small;
For the dear God who loveth us,
He made and loveth all.

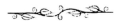

William Cowper (1731-1800), English Poet

Beware of desperate steps; the darkest day lived till tomorrow will have passed   away.

The Rev. Maurice McCrackin (1905-1997)

Let us foster a united community, free from discrimination - a city that may be called a 'beloved community' which provides equal justice for all.

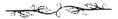

James Cromwell (born 1940), English Actor in the Cinema Movie Babe

Pigs may not be as cuddly as kittens or puppies, but they suffer just as much.

James Cromwell (born 1940), English Actor in the film Babe

We don't need to eat anyone who would run, swim, or fly away if he could.

Mary Daly

> Rapism: the fundamental ideology and practice of patriarchy,
> characterized by invasion, violation, degradation,
> objectification, and destruction of women and nature;
> the fundamental paradigm of racism, classism,
> and all the other oppressive-isms. [Animals live on rape racks!]

L. T. Danshiell, Animal Rights Advocate

> Show me the enforced laws of a state for the prevention of cruelty
> to animals and I in turn will give you a correct estimate of the
> refinement, enlightenment, integrity and equity of that
> commonwealth's people.

Charles Darwin (1809-1882), English Scientist
> The most energetic workers I have encountered in my world
> travels are the vegetarian miners of Chile.

Charles Darwin (1809-1882), English Scientist

There is no fundamental difference between man and the higher mammals in their mental faculties ... The difference in mind between man and the higher animals, great as it is, certainly is one of degree and not of kind. The love for all living creatures is the most noble attribute of man. We have seen that the senses and intuitions, the various emotions and faculties, such as love, memory, attention and curiosity, imitation, reason, etc., of which man boasts, may be found in an incipient, or even sometimes a well-developed condition, in the lower animals.

Charles Darwin (1809-1882), English Scientist

As man advanced gradually in intellectual power and was enabled to trace the more remote consequences of his actions; as his sympathies became more tender and widely diffused, extending to men of all races, and finally, to the lower animals, so would the standard of his morality rise higher and higher.

Robertson Davies

The dog is a yes-animal, very popular with people who can't afford to keep a yes-man.

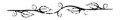

Leonardo Da Vinci (1452-1519), Italian Genius, Painter, Sculptor, Architect, Engineer and Scientist

The time will come when men such as I will look upon the murder of animals as they now look upon the murder of men.

Herman Daggett, Christian Minister ~ The Rights of Animals, His Oration, in in Rhode Island, USA (1791)

The design of my appearing in public, at this time, is to say a few things in favor of a certain class of beings whose rights have seldom been advocated, either from the pulpit, from the stage, or from the press. I mean the inferior animals.

The cruelty and injustice with which this class of beings has been treated by their boasted superiors of the human race is too notorious to need a particular recital. In general, their welfare and happiness has been looked upon as a matter of very little importance in the system, and in our treatment of them, hardly to be regarded....

That they are sensible beings and capable of happiness, none can doubt: That their sensibility of corporeal pleasure and pain is less than ours, none can prove: And that there is any kind of reason why they should not be regarded with proportionable tenderness, we cannot conceive.

But lest this mode of reasoning should be thought too nice, let us call into view a rule of judging, instituted by a divine Philanthropist and oracle of wisdom in the days of Julius (Tiberius) Caesar. 'That we do to others as we would have them do unto us.'

Whereas there is no such consciousness of guilt when one of the inferior animals only has been the subject of human cruelty,...let a person be taught from his earliest years that it is criminal to torment and unnecessarily to destroy these innocent animals, and he will feel a guilty conscience..

Leonardo Da Vinci (1452-1519), Italian Genius, Painter, Sculptor, Architect, Engineer and Scientist

My body will not be a tomb for other creatures.

Leonardo Da Vinci (1452-1519), Italian Genius, Painter, Sculptor, Architect, Engineer and Scientist Truly man is the king of beasts, for his brutality exceeds theirs. We live by the death of others: We are burial places!

Leonardo Da Vinci (1452-1519), Italian Genius, Painter, Sculptor, Architect, Engineer and Scientist

I have from an early age abjured the use of meat and the time will come when men   such as I will look upon the murder of animals as they now look upon the murder of men.

Leonardo Da Vinci (1452-1519), Italian Genius, Painter, Sculptor, Architect, Engineer and Scientist

The smallest feline is a masterpiece.

Karen Davis, PhD., President and Founder of United Poultry Concerns (UPC)

Can one regard a fellow creature as a property item, an investment, a piece of meat, an 'it,' without degenerating into cruelty towards that creature?

Michel De Montaigne (1533-1592), French Essayist

For my part I have never been able to see, without displeasure, an innocent and   defenseless animal, from whom we receive no offense or harm, pursued and   slaughtered.

Harvey Diamond, American Author: Co-Author of Fit for Life

You put a baby in a crib with an apple and a rabbit. If it eats the rabbit and plays with the apple, I'll buy you a new car.

Gregory Dick (Born 1932), American Comedian

Martin Luther King taught us all nonviolence. I was told to extend it to the mother and her calf.

Cameron Diaz, American Actress

Many years ago when Cameron Diaz learned that pigs have the same mental capacity/intelligence as 3 year old human children she stopped eating pigs in contrast to her pork- eating half-Cuban background.Revolted she said: 'My niece was three at the time, which is a magical age, I thought,Oh, my God; it's like eating my niece!'

Diogenes (412-323 BC), Greek Philosopher

We might as well eat the flesh of men as the flesh of other animals.

Luke A Dommer

Today's wildlife management philosophy is based on propagating game animal populations for the sole purpose of increasing hunter recreation. Prescribed burning or clear-cutting of forests to promote more game animals necessarily results in the...deterioration of biological diversity.

Robert Donjacour

I fail to understand why teaching kids not to eat meat and not to kill animals (which I think is teaching respect for life) is considered coercion, whereas teaching them to eat meat, etc. is not.

Fyodor Dostoyevsky (1821-1881), Russian Author

Love the world with an all-embracing love. Love the animals; God has given them the rudiments of thought and joy untroubled. Do not trouble them, do not harass then, do not deprive them of their happiness, and do not work against God's intent. Man, do not pride yourself on your superiority to them, for they are without sin, and you with your greatness defile the earth.

Fyodor Dostoyevsky (1821-1881), Russian Author: From The Brothers Karamazov, 1880

Love the animals, love the plants, love everything. If you love everything, you will perceive the divine mystery in things. Once you perceive it, you will begin to comprehend it better every day. And you will come to love the whole world with an all-embracing love.

Fyodor Dostoyevsky (1821-1881), Russian Author

Imagine that you are creating a fabric of human destiny with the object of making men happy in the end... but that it was essential and inevitable to torture to death only one tiny creature... And to found that edifice on its unavenged tears: would you consent to be the architect on those conditions? Tell me, and tell me the truth!

Fyodor Dostoyevsky (1821-1881), Russian Author

Love animals: God has given them the rudiments of thought and joy untroubled. Do not trouble their joy, don't harass them, and don't deprive them of their happiness.

Don't work against God's intent. Man, do not pride yourself on superiority to animals; they are without sin, and you, with your greatness, defile the earth by your appearance on it, and leave the traces of your foulness after you - alas, it is true of almost every one of us!

Fyodor Dostoyevsky (1821-1881), Russian Author

Love all God's creatures, the animals, the plants. Love everything to perceive the divine mystery in all.

Fyodor Dostoyevsky (1821-1881), Russian Author

It is not possible to eat me without insisting that I sing praises of my devourer?

Fyodor Dostoyevsky (1821-1881), Russian Author

Imagine that you are creating a fabric of human destiny with the object of making men happy in the end...but that it was essential and inevitable to torture to death only one tiny creature... And to found that edifice on its unavenged tears: would you consent to be the architect on those conditions? Tell me, and tell me the truth!

Fyodor Dostoyevsky (1821-1881), Russian Author

Men do not accept their prophets and slay them, but they love their martyrs and worship those whom they have tortured to death.

Fyodor Dostoyevsky (1821-1881), Russian Author

To live without hope is to cease to live.

Fyodor Dostoyevsky (1821-1881), Russian Author

To love someone means to see him as God intended him.

Lord Hugh Dowding, Founder of The Lord Dowding Fund for Humane Research: Delivered to the House of Lords, 1957

I firmly believe that painful experiments on animals are morally wrong, and that it is basically immoral to do evil in order that good may come – even if it were proved that mankind benefits from the suffering inflicted on animals. I further believe that, in the vast majority of cases, mankind does not so benefit and the results of vivisection are, in fact, misleading and harmful.

Max Eastman: Enjoyment of Laughter

Dogs laugh, but they laugh with their tails.

Meister Eckhart (1260-1327), German Theologian

Apprehend God in all things, for God is in all things. Every single creature is full of God and is a book about God. Every creature is a word of God.

Ecclesiastes 3:19

Ecclesiastes 3:19: Tells us that the vicissitudes of life affect human and non-human animals alike, both know suffering and ultimately die, both possess and share the same breath/life/soul and that humankind should not consider themselves superior to their animal brethren nor dominate them: For that which befalleth the sons of men befallest beasts...As one dieth, so dieth the other. Yet they have all one breath...[and] a man hath no pre-eminence over a beast.

Mark Edgemon

Know your limitations...then plow right through them!

Mark Edgemon

Presumption by a competent person is innovation; presumption by a fool is courting destruction.

Mark Edgemon

Life is a journey...not a destination!

Mark Edgemon

Never give anyone control over your vision!

Mark Edgemon

Following your own inspiration, produces a work that is real and is not affected by the influences of what others might think, which leads to creative freedom!

Mark Edgemon

If the answer is not a yes...it's a no! [Make a decision and stick by it.]

Mark Edgemon

Never give leeway...the righteous don't need it and the wicked don't deserve it.

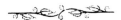

Mark Edgemon

Never let a person hold your happiness hostage. [We should not deny happiness to animals.]

Mark Edgemon

The simplest truths are the hardest to understand. [Vegetarianism is at the lost core of most religious teachings- so simple yet denied distorted and lost.]

Mark Edgemon

People, who seek virtue, must have the courage to pursue it!

Mark Edgemon

Life is a process...not an end result!

Mark Edgemon

Gratitude is short for a great attitude!

Mark Edgemon

When I'm losing, I fight with all my might. When I'm winning, I fight even harder!

Mark Edgemon

Never hope against hope...there's no hope in it!

Mark Edgemon

No one conquers who doesn't fight! [Follow your principles.]

Mark Edgemon

Compassion is merited, by one's degree of humility.

Albert Einstein (1879-1955), Famous Scientist and Educator

The important thing is not to stop questioning.

Thomas Edison (1847-1931), Inventor

Non-violence leads to the highest ethics, which is the goal of all evolution. Until we stop harming ALL other living beings, we are still savages.

Thomas Edison (1847-1931), Inventor

The doctor of the future will no longer treat the human frame with drugs, but rather will cure and prevent disease with nutrition!!

Albert Einstein (1879-1955), Famous Scientist and Educator

Nothing will benefit human health and increase chances for survival of life on Earth as much as the evolution to a vegetarian diet.

Albert Einstein (1879-1955), Famous Scientist and Educator

Our task must be to free ourselves...by widening our circle of compassion to embrace all living creatures and the whole of nature and its beauty.

Albert Einstein (1879-1955), Famous Scientist and Educator

Try not to become a person of success, but try instead to become a person of value.

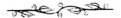

Albert Einstein (1879-1955), Famous Scientist and Educator

The man who regards his own life and that of his fellow creatures as meaningless is not merely unhappy but hardly fit for life.

Albert Einstein (1879-1955), Famous Scientist & Educator

Vegetarian food leaves a deep impression on our nature. If the whole world adopts vegetarianism, it can change the destiny of humankind.

Dwight D. Eisenhower, President of the United States

Every gun that is made, every warship launched, every rocket fired signifies, in the final sense, a theft from those who hunger and are not fed, those who are cold and are not clothed. This world in arms is not spending money alone. It is spending the sweat of its laborers, the genius of its scientists, the hopes of its children ... Under the cloud of threatening war; it is humanity hanging from a cross of iron.

George Eisman, Registered Dietitian, Author ~ From Incredibly Delicious, by Gentle World, (P114)

Most nutrition professionals agree that moving away from an animal product-based diet to a plant-based diet is the single most important improvement Americans (and others who eat similarly) can do to improve their well-being. I personally have eaten vegan (totally vegetarian) for over 15 years and have raised my two children that way since birth.

George Eliot

We long for an affection altogether ignorant of our faults. Heaven has accorded this to us in the uncritical canine attachment.

Black Elk

We should understand well that all things are the work of the Great Spirit. We should know the Great Spirit is within all things: the trees, the grasses, the rivers, the mountains, and the four-legged and winged peoples; and even more important, we should understand that the Great Spirit is also above all these things and peoples. When we do understand all this deeply in our hearts, then we will fear, and love, and know the Great Spirit, and then we will be and act and live as the Spirit intends.

Bob Ekstrom

Tongue - a variety of meat, rarely served because it clearly crosses the line between a cut of beef and a piece of a dead cow.

Ralph Waldo Emerson (1803-1882), American Philosopher, Poet and Essayist

You have just dined, and however scrupulously the slaughterhouse is concealed in the graceful distance of miles, there is complicity.

Ralph Waldo Emerson (1803-1882), American Philosopher, Poet and Essayist: Closing lines of his Essay on: Self-Reliance

A political victory, a rise of rents, the recovery of your sick, or the return of your absent friend, or some other favorable event, raises your spirits, and you think good days are preparing for you. Do not believe it. Nothing can bring you peace but yourself. Nothing can bring you peace but the triumph of your principles.

Ralph Waldo Emerson (1803-1882), American Philosopher, Poet and Essayist

What is a weed? A plant whose virtues have never been discovered.

Ralph Waldo Emerson (1803-1882), American Philosopher, Poet and Essayist

A more secret, sweet, and overpowering beauty appears to man when his heart and mind open to the sentiment of virtue. Then he is instructed in what is above him. He learns that his being is without bound; that to the good, to the perfect, his is born.

Ralph Waldo Emerson (1803-1882), American Philosopher, Poet and Essayist

Plato [the vegetarian] is philosophy, and philosophy is Plato...Out of Plato come all things that are still written and debated among men of thought.

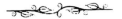

Ralph Waldo Emerson (1803-1882), American Philosopher, Poet and Essayist

Poetry must be new as foam, and as old as the rock.

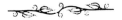

Ralph Waldo Emerson (1803-1882), American Philosopher, Poet and Essayist

Poetry teaches the enormous force of a few words, and, in proportion to the inspiration, checks loquacity.

Ralph Waldo Emerson (1803-1882), American Philosopher, Poet and Essayist

> You have just dined, and however scrupulously the slaughterhouse is concealed in the graceful distance of miles, there is complicity.

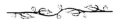

Ralph Waldo Emerson (1803-1882), American Philosopher, Poet and Essayist

> Do not go where the path may lead, go instead where there is no path and leave a trail. [Follow virtue.]

Ralph Waldo Emerson (1803-1882), American Philosopher, Poet and Essayist

> All I have seen teaches me to trust the Creator for all I have not seen.

Ralph Waldo Emerson (1803-1882), American Philosopher, Poet and Essayist

> Character is higher than intellect... A great soul will be strong to live, as well as to think.

Ralph Waldo Emerson (1803-1882), American Philosopher, Poet & Essayist

> A friend is one before whom I may think aloud.

Ralph Waldo Emerson (1803-1882), American Philosopher, Poet and Essayist

Be not the slave of your own past. Plunge into the sublime seas, dive deep and swim far, so you shall come back with self-respect, with new power, with an advanced experience that shall explain and overlook the old. [Stand by your moral choices.]

Ralph Waldo Emerson (1803-1882), American Philosopher, Poet & Essayist

The reward of a thing well done is to have done it.

Ralph Waldo Emerson (1803-1882), American Philosopher, Poet & Essayist

A hero is no braver than an ordinary man, but he is braver five minutes longer.

Lord Thomas Erskine (1750-1823)

I am to ask you're Lordships, in the name of that God who gave to man his dominion over the lower world, to acknowledge and recognize that dominion to be a moral trust.

The Essene Gospel of Peace

And the flesh of the slain beasts in his body will become his own tomb. For I tell you truly, he who kills kills himself and he who eats the flesh of slain beasts, eats the body of death.

George Bird Evans: Troubles with Bird Dogs

I think we are drawn to dogs because they are the uninhibited creatures we might be if we weren't certain we knew better. They fight for honor at the first challenge, make love with no moral restraint, and they do not for all their marvelous instincts appear to know about death. Being such wonderfully uncomplicated beings, they need us to do their worrying.

Jon Evans (1917-)

To inflict cruelties on defenseless creatures, or condone such acts, is to abuse one of the cardinal tenets of a civilized society - Reverence for Life.

Ezekiel 3:4 (Judaism and Christianity)

My body has never been defiled by animal flesh.

Elizabeth Jane Farians PhD.

Just as there cannot be peace without justice,
So there cannot be peace without compassion
For every living thing, because the human heart
Can tolerate neither injustice nor cruelty.

Elizabeth Jane Farians PhD.

To try to picture the Christ, the one whom Christians call 'Agnus Dei,' the Lamb of God, chewing on a leg of lamb seems incongruous to me.

Elizabeth Jane Farians PhD.

May you and every living thing be embraced in the arms of compassion...

Elizabeth Jane Farians PhD.

Let us, each one,
Dance lightly with the living earth
Respecting:
One's self - body and mind
Each person and all peoples
All of the animals and every sentient being,
The environment and every living thing.

Eugene Field: The Love Affairs of a Bibliomaniac

Yet there have been, and there still are, many who take a seeming delight in telling you how many conquests they have made, and they not infrequently have the bad taste to explain with wearisome prolixity the ways and the means whereby those conquests were wrought; as, forsooth, an unfeeling huntsman is forever boasting of the game he has slaughtered and is forever dilating upon the repulsive details of his butcheries.

Eugene Field: The Love Affairs of a Bibliomaniac

The best anglers in the world are those who do not catch fish; the mere slaughter of fish is simply brutal....

Charles Fillmore, Co-founder of The Unity Society of Practical Christianity: On Diet, Health and Vegetarianism: From: As to Meat Eating, 1903

I was shown that the food that entered the organism had to pass through a process of regeneration every day before it was in condition to be built into the new body of Christ.

Charles Fillmore, Co-founder of The Unity Society of Practical Christianity: On Diet, Health and Vegetarianism: From: As to Meat Eating, 1903

If we are eating aggregations of life ideas hid within the material forms, we should use discrimination in choosing those forms. Our food should be full of life in its purity and vigor. There should be no idea of death and decay connected with it in any degree. The vegetable should be fresh and the fruit radiant in its sunny perfection.

Charles Fillmore, Co-founder of The Unity Society of Practical Christianity: On Diet, Health and Vegetarianism: From: As to Meat Eating, 1903

We eat the flesh of the animal for the life it contains, yet the fact is that life has disappeared in its highest degree---there is left only a lot of corpse cells in various stages of corruption and decay. These are really a burden to the organism...Yet ignorant man loads his system with these elements of discord and decay and expects to get life out of them.

Charles Fillmore, Co-founder of The Unity Society of Practical Christianity: On Diet, Health and Vegetarianism: From: Flesh-Eating Metaphysically Considered, 1910

The master on the spiritual plane is not a slave driver...He must love every creature...His love must flow forth in protecting streams when any creature is in danger of violence or destruction. He must recognize all life as God's life...Thus he cannot in any way sanction the killing of animals for food, nor can he give passive assent by eating the flesh of those slain by the hands of ignorant man.

Charles Fillmore, Co-founder of The Unity Society of Practical Christianity: On Diet, Health and Vegetarianism: From: Flesh-Eating Metaphysically Considered, 1910

> He who eats the flesh of animals is, by and through that process, taking into his consciousness all the passions, desires, and emotions of animals. Do not deceive yourself...that it makes no difference what you eat. There is no absence of life, substance, or intelligence anywhere.

Charles Fillmore, Co-founder of The Unity Society of Practical Christianity: On Diet, Health and Vegetarianism: From: Flesh-Eating Metaphysically Considered, 1910

> In eating the flesh of animals, we are feeding and stimulating the animal mentality that pervades our bodies. Instead of transforming the flesh consciousness into Spirit, we are adding to its power to bind us to the plane of sensation.

Charles Fillmore, Co-founder of The Unity Society of Practical Christianity: On Diet, Health and Vegetarianism: From: Vegetarianism, 1915

> It was the custom of Jesus to use familiar things for his illustrations, and as the people he worked among were fishermen, it was but natural that fish should figure prominently as illustrations in this teaching. Instead of trying to change the customs of the people, he laid down certain universal principles which would lead the people themselves to change their customs. He knew that mere outward conformity to righteousness did not fulfill the divine Law which requires man to choose for himself the principles of Truth and work them out in his own life. One of these principles is Love Universal.

Charles Fillmore, Co-founder of The Unity Society of Practical Christianity: On Diet, Health and Vegetarianism: From: The Vegetarian, 1915

On one occasion, Jesus said to his disciples, 'I have many things to say unto you, but ye cannot bear them now.' When he was in Palestine, the race was not ready for the great revolution that was to accompany the ushering in of the new race and the earth...He did not try to explain to them the detail of 'the restitution of all things'...Now the understanding that life and love are to be demonstrated is becoming general...Therefore, in the light of the Truth that God is love, and that Jesus came to make his love manifest in the world, we cannot believe it is his will for men to eat meat, or to do anything else that would cause suffering to the innocent and helpless.

Charles Fillmore, Co-founder of The Unity Society of Practical Christianity: On Diet, Health and Vegetarianism: From: Eating and Drinking, 1931

The invisible psychic agony of millions of cruelly slaughtered animals saturates our earth's atmosphere and the whole race suffers in sympathy. We make intimate mental contact with these psychic terrors of our little sisters and brothers of the animal world when we devour their fear-shattered bodies. Out vague fear of impending danger, our troubled sleep, our dread of the future, and numerous other unidentified mental complexes may and often are the echo fears of the brutes whose flesh we have entombed in our stomach.

Corey Ford

Properly trained, a man can be dog's best friend.

Charles Fillmore, Co-founder of The Unity Society of Practical Christianity: On Diet, Health and Vegetarianism: From: The Vegetarian, 1920

Spirit has shown me repeatedly that I could not refine my body and make it a harmonious instrument for the soul, so long as I continued to fill it with the cells of dead animals.

Charles Fillmore, Co-founder of The Unity Society of Practical Christianity: On Diet, Health and Vegetarianism: From: Eating and Drinking, 1931

Physiologists tell us that beefsteak is a stimulant, and that people get intoxicated with meat eating. Some persons become intoxicated with coffee and tea; others with cocoa. All these things have an intoxicating effect, and the system, if you cultivate it in that direction, will keep calling more for such stimulants.

Charles Fillmore, Co-founder of The Unity Society of Practical Christianity: On Diet, Health and Vegetarianism: From: The Vegetarian, 1920

We need never look for universal peace on this earth until men stop killing animals for food.

Charles Fillmore, Co-founder of The Unity Society of Practical Christianity: On Diet, Health and Vegetarianism: From: The Vegetarian, 1920

Undoubtedly the next great step forward in the reformation and refinement of humanity will be the elimination of flesh food. We do not anticipate a world-wide prohibition but a gradual adaptation of the best foods by progressive people.

Charles Fillmore, Co-founder of The Unity Society of Practical Christianity: On Diet, Health and Vegetarianism: From: Eating and Drinking, 1931

> If you find that you are a victim of the desire for stimulant in any of its forms, say to the appetite: 'I no longer desire those things; I am no longer hypnotized or mesmerized by sense appetite...My stimulant is Spirit, and I desire the stimulants of Spirit only. I live in the life, the quickening energy, and the power of the Spirit.

Charles Fillmore, Co-founder of Unity Society of Practical Christianity, on Diet, Health and Vegetarianism: From: Eating and Drinking, 1931

> We know that the drinking of intoxicants and the using of tobacco in any form are dissipations of force. The natural energies of man are set aside when he looks to stimulants of any kind as the source of life.

Lancelot, Fleming, (Bishop of Norwich), Extract from: The Living World, Vol.1, No.2: Crusade Against All Cruelty to Animals, 1970
> We speak of human rights. I think we should also speak of animal rights and natural rights, but there must be some radical re-orientation in current attitudes and thinking before these rights are recognized and respected.

Diane Fossey (1932-1985), American Zoologist who observed eight gorilla groups in the mountain forests of Rwanda. She was murdered by animal killers.

> The man who kills the animals today is the man who kills the people who get in his way tomorrow.

Carol Tucker Foreman: Assistant Secretary of Agriculture (President Carter's Administration): Commenting on the inadequacy of the U.S. Department of Agriculture's Streamlined (Meat) Inspection System (SIS)

> The thousands of people who have suffered food poisoning after eating beef will, no doubt, appreciate that their beef was aesthetically acceptable, even though it made them ill. 'Lovely to look at, dangerous to eat' is not a standard that is likely to help beef sales.

Anatole France (1844-1924), French Author and Critic

> If 50 million people say a foolish thing, it is still a foolish thing.

Richard J Foster, Professor of Theology: Celebration of Discipline: The Path to Spiritual Growth, Revised Edition, New York, Harper & Row, 1988, (P91)

> Simplicity is freedom, not slavery. Refuse to be a slave to anything but God.

Anatole France (1844-1924), French Author and Critic

> Until one has loved an animal, a part of one's soul remains unawakened.

Gary Francione, Lawyer, Professor and Author

> The best justification we have for inflicting pain, suffering and death on 10 billion animals a year is that they taste good. I regard that as moral schizophrenia.

James Anthony Froude

Wild animals never kill for sport. Man is the only one to whom the torture and death of his fellow-creatures is amusing in itself.

Gary Francione, Lawyer, Professor and Author

The most important thing anyone can do is to become vegan and to educate others about why taking animals seriously means being vegan. As more and more people become vegan, demand drops and consciousness about the immoral and unjustifiable nature of animal use is raised. I regard veganism as the most important form of activism for nonhuman animals. Veganism is the principle of abolition applied to the life of the individual.

Benjamin Franklin (1706-1790), Printer, Author, Publisher, Inventor, Scientist, Businessman, Philosopher, Statesman and Diplomat

My refusing to eat meat occasioned inconveniency, and I have been frequently chided for my singularity. But my light repast allows for greater progress, for greater clearness of head and quicker comprehension.

Benjamin Franklin (1706-1790), Printer, Author, Publisher, Inventor, Scientist, Businessman, Philosopher, Statesman and Diplomat

A man who gives up some of his freedom in pursuit of security deserves neither security nor freedom!

Benjamin Franklin (1706-1790), Printer, Author, Publisher, Inventor, Scientist, Businessman, Philosopher, Statesman and Diplomat

Flesh eating is unprovoked murder.

Edward Augustus Freeman (1823-1892) British Historian and Commentator

The awful wrongs and sufferings forced upon the innocent, helpless, faithful animal race form the blackest chapter in the whole world's history.

Fruitarian Network

Objectification reduces sensitivity. Thus cows are called beef or head of cattle, pigs become pork, sheep mutton. The screams are muted... and living creatures become plastic wrapped packages.

Roy Fuller (1912-1991) English Poet and Novelist

It is man who has fallen, not the beasts: that is the message even for the irreligious, and to some extent salvation can be measured by his very treatment of them.

Thomas Fuller (1608-1661) English Clergyman and Historian
If it were not for hope, the heart would break.

Thomas Fuller (1608-1661) English Clergyman and Historian

The great end of life is not knowledge, but action. [Stand by your ethical principles]

Thomas Fuller (1608-1661) English Clergyman and Historian

He that will not be merciful to his beast is a beast himself.

Galileo Galilei, (1564-1642)

I do not feel obliged to believe that the same God who has endowed us with sense, reason, and intellect has intended us to forgo their use.

John Galsworthy (1867-1933), English Writer Extract from: Much Cry, Little Wool

Once admit that we have the right to inflict unnecessary suffering and you destroy the very basis of human society.

Mahatma Gandhi (1869-1948), Hindu Pacifist, Nationalist Leader and Social Reformer

I want to realize brotherhood or identity
Not merely with the beings called human,
But I want to realize identity with all life,
Even with such things as crawl upon earth.

Mahatma Gandhi (1869-1948), Hindu Pacifist, Nationalist Leader and Social Reformer

It is very significant that some of the most thoughtful and cultured men are partisans of a pure vegetable diet.

Mahatma Gandhi (1869-1948), Hindu Pacifist, Nationalist Leader and Social Reformer

I do not regard flesh-food as necessary for us at any stage and under any clime in which it is possible for human beings ordinarily to live, I hold flesh-food to be unsuited to our species. To my mind, the life of a lamb is no less precious than that of a human being. I should be unwilling to take the life of a lamb for the sake of the human body. I hold that, the more helpless a creature, the more entitled it is to the protection by man from the cruelty of man.

Mahatma Gandhi (1869-1948), Hindu Pacifist, Nationalist Leader and Social Reformer

I abhor vivisection with my whole soul. All the scientific discoveries stained with innocent blood I count as of no consequence.

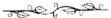

Mohandas Gandhi (1869-1948), Hindu Pacifist, Nationalist Leader and Social Reformer

The greatness of a nation and its moral progress can be judged by the way its animals are treated.

Mohandas Gandhi (1869-1948), Hindu Pacifist, Nationalist Leader and Social Reformer

The only way to live is to let live.

Mohandas Gandhi (1869-1948), Hindu Pacifist, Nationalist Leader and Social Reformer

I do not regard flesh food as necessary for us. I hold flesh food to be unsuited to our species. We err in copying the lower animal world if we are superior to it.

Mohandas Gandhi (1869-1948), Hindu Pacifist, Nationalist Leader and Social Reformer

In a gentle way you can shake the world.

Mohandas Gandhi (1869-1948), Hindu Pacifist, Nationalist Leader and Social Reformer

It ill becomes us to invoke in our daily prayers the blessings of God, the Compassionate, if we in turn will not practice elementary compassion toward our fellow creatures.

Mohandas Gandhi (1869-1948), Hindu Pacifist, Nationalist Leader and Social Reformer

I have learned through bitter experience the one supreme lesson to conserve my anger, and as heat conserved is transmitted into energy, even so our anger controlled can be transmitted into a power that can move the world.

Mohandas Gandhi (1869-1948), Hindu Pacifist, Nationalist Leader and Social Reformer

I do feel that spiritual progress does demand at some stage that we should cease to kill our fellow creatures for the satisfaction of our bodily wants.

Mohandas Gandhi (1869-1948), Hindu Pacifist, Nationalist Leader and Social Reformer

Vivisection is the blackest of all the black crimes that man is at present committing against God and his animal creations.

Mohandas Gandhi (1869-1948), Hindu Pacifist, Nationalist Leader and Social Reformer

An eye for an eye and the whole world goes blind.

R. Garaudy

The greatest cultural revolution of all times (will be)
One which replaces a structure and culture that has
Been worked out by the male half of humankind
Over thousands of years by a structure and culture
That will be the handiwork of the whole of humankind
Comprising the female as well as the male.
[We should introduce universal compassion]

Alberto Giacometti

In a burning building I would save a cat before a Rembrandt.

Richard Gere, Actor

As custodians of the planet it is our responsibility to deal with all species with kindness, love, and compassion. That these animals suffer through human cruelty is beyond understanding. Please help to stop this madness.

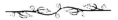

Extract from: The Book of Genesis (Jewish and Christian Scriptures)

And God said, Behold, I have given you every herb bearing seed, which is upon the face of all the earth, and every tree, in which is the fruit of a tree yielding seed; to you it shall be for meat. And to every beast of the earth, and to every fowl of the air, and to everything that creepeth upon the earth, wherein there is life, I have given every green herb for meat; and it was so.

God, Isaiah 1:111:15-16 (Judaism and Christianity)

Of what use are all your sacrifices to Me? I have had enough of the roasted carcasses of rams and of the fat of fattened beasts. I take no pleasure in the blood of calves, lambs and goats. When you spread out your hands, I close My eyes to you; despite however much you pray, I will not listen. Your hands are full of blood! Wash yourselves clean! Put away your misdeeds from before My eyes and stop doing evil.

Jane Goodall, The Jane Goodall Institute

Farm animals feel pleasure and sadness, excitement and resentment, depression, fear, and pain. They are far more aware and intelligent than we ever imagined...they are individuals in their own right.

Sir Wilfred Grenfell (1865-1940): The Adventure of Life

Kindness to all God's creatures is an absolute rock-bottom
necessity if peace and righteousness are to prevail.

Elizabeth Goudge (1900-1984)

Nothing living should ever be treated with contempt. Whatever
it is that lives, a man, a tree, or a bird, should be touched gently,
because the time is short. Civilization is another word for respect
for life...

Temple Grandin PhD, Board Member of U.S.A. meat industry's Livestock Conservation Institute & Assistant Professor of Animal Science at Colorado State University

Killing an animal is not the same thing as mowing the grass. A life
ends. That's something you take seriously. What does the word
'sacred' mean? You do not treat it as an ordinary thing. Killing
cattle is not the same as running grain through a mill.

Dick Gregory: In 1968 as the Civil Rights Leader he compared humanity's treatment of animals with the conditions of America's inner cities

Animals and humans suffer and die alike. If you had on kill your
own hog before you ate it, most likely you would not be able to do
it. To hear the hog scream, to see the blood spill, to see the baby
being taken away from its momma, and to see the look of death in
the animals eye would turn your stomach. So you get the man at
the packing house to do the killing for you.

Temple Grandin PhD, Board Member of U.S.A. Meat Industry's Livestock Conservation Institute and Assistant Professor of Animal Science at Colorado State University, USA

> That's one sad, unhappy, upset cow. She wants her baby.
> Bellowing for [her baby], hunting for [her baby] it. It's like
> grieving, mourning - not much written about it. People don't like
> to allow them thought or feelings.
> [Few cow-flesh eaters know that all cows clearly and distinctly
> react in a frantic, panicked, broken-hearted manner for many
> weeks after their babies are taken away and cramped into small,
> dark crates, without light and companionship, later to be
> butchered, sliced and sold as veal. Finally, their mothers, hoarse,
> rasping without voices, out of their minds with grief, their
> emotions and souls are most evidently and painstakingly broken].

Dick Gregory: In 1968 as the Civil Rights Leader he compared humanity's treatment of animals with the conditions of America's inner cities

> In like manner, if the wealthy aristocrats who are perpetrating
> conditions in the ghetto actually heard the screams of ghetto
> suffering, or saw the slow death of hungry little kids, or witnessed
> the strangulation of manhood and dignity, they could not
> continue the killing. But the wealthy are protected from such
> horror...If you can justify killing to eat meat, you can justify the
> conditions of the ghetto. I cannot justify either one.

Robert Grillo

What we leave behind - our legacy - is how we affected others. And for most of us, no other choice has a greater impact on the legacy of help - or harm - we leave behind, than our daily food choices. Day after day, and year after year, our lives can be seen as the culmination of thousands of instances in which, equally assured of nourishment and health, we had the opportunity to choose kindness and mercy toward other animals, or to choose violence and death for them.

For billions of people, the question of eating animals really comes down to this basic question: am I someone who, when able to freely choose, would rather harm animals, or help them?

When able to choose, do I choose kindness over violence or violence over kindness? Our answer is our legacy."

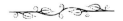

Ruth Harrison

If one person is unkind to an animal, it is considered to be cruelty, but where a lot of people are unkind to animals, especially in the name of commerce, the cruelty is condoned and once sums of money are at stake, will be defended to the last by otherwise intelligent people.

Hadith - Teachings and Sayings of the Prophet Muhammad: Islam

A good deed done to an animal is as meritorious as a good deed done to a human being, while an act of cruelty to an animal is a bad as an act of cruelty to a human being.

Paul Harvey (1918-2009), American Radio Commentator

Ever occur to you why some of us can be this much concerned with animals' suffering? Because government is not. Why not? Animals don't vote.

Paul Harvey (1918-2009), American Radio Commentator

...Dickensian compassion rescued children from sweat shops. Lincolnian empathy rescued slaves from being 'things'. Civilization weeps while it awaits one more emancipation.

Nathaniel Hawthorne (1804-1864), Author

...and we have so far improved upon the custom of Adam and Eve, that we generally furnish forth our feasts with a portion of some delicate calf or lamb, whose unspotted innocence entitles them to the happiness of becoming our sustenance.

Hesiod, Greek Poet (c. 700 BC)

He harms himself who does harm to another, and the evil plan is most harmful to the planner.

Cardinal Heenan, Foreword to God's Animals by Ambrose Agius: Catholic Study Circle for Animal Welfare, 1970

Animals have very positive rights because they are God's creatures. If we have to speak with absolute accuracy we must say that God has the right to have all his creatures treated with proper respect.

James Herriot (1916-1995), British Veterinarian and Author: His first two novels were compiled into the volume: All Creatures Great and Small.

> If having a soul means being able to feel love and loyalty and gratitude, then animals are better off than a lot of humans.

Alex Hershaft, Founder, Farm Animal Reform Movement (FARM), 1982

> My friends, it is so much easier to look four years ahead if you can look 40 years back, as I can. We are winning. Yes, it is dreadfully slow from a one-year perspective, and it will continue to be from a one-year perspective. But it is pretty amazing from a 40-year perspective.

Hinduism, Manusmriti 5.49

> Having well considered the origin of flesh foods. And the cruelty of fettering and slaying corporeal beings let man entirely abstain from eating flesh.

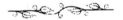

Hieronymus (331-420): Adversus Jovinanum 1:30: Prophetic Words Against the Sinful Biblical Sacrifice of Animals and Against Eating Animal Flesh

> The consumption of animal flesh was unknown up until the Great Flood. But since the Great Flood, we have had the fibres and the stinking fluids of animal flesh stuffed into our mouths...Jesus, the Christ, who appeared when the time was fulfilled, again joined the end to the beginning, so that we are now no longer allowed to eat animal flesh.

Hinduism, Upanishads

What is religion? Compassion for all things, which have life.

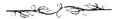

Hippocrates (460 BC-377 BC)

The soul is the same in all living creatures, although the body of each is different.

Edward Hoagland

In order to really enjoy a dog, one doesn't merely try to train him to be semi human. The point of it is to open oneself to the possibility of becoming partly a dog.

Rabbi Samson Rafael Hirsch (1808-1888), Father of German Jewish Orthodoxy and Chief Rabbi of Austria. Excerpt from Horeb: Chapter 72, Section 482

Here you are faced with God's teaching, which obliges you not only to refrain from inflicting unnecessary pain on any animal, but to help and, when you can, to lessen the pain whenever you see an animal suffering, even through no fault of yours....As God is merciful, and so you also be merciful.

As he loved and cares for all His creatures and His children and are related to Him, because He is their Father, so you also love all His creatures as your brethren. Let their joys be your joys, and their sorrows yours. Love them and with every power which God gives you, work for their welfare and benefit, because they are the children of your God, because they are your brothers and sisters.

His Holiness the XIV Dalai Lama of Tibet (Born 1935)

In order to satisfy one human stomach, so many lives are taken away. We must promote vegetarianism, It is extremely important.

His Holiness the XIV Dalai Lama of Tibet (Born 1935)

Whenever I visit a market and see the chickens crowded together in tiny cages that give them no room to move around and spread their wings and the fish slowly drowning in the air, my heart goes out to them. People have to learn to think about animals in a different way, as sentient beings who love life and fear death. I urge everyone who can to adopt a compassionate vegetarian diet.

His Holiness the XIV Dalai Lama of Tibet (Born 1935): Speaking at the World Vegetarian Congress, 1967

In our approach to life, be it pragmatic or otherwise, the ultimate truth that confronts us squarely and unmistakably is the desire for peace, security and happiness. Different forms of life in different aspects of existence make up the teeming denizens of this earth of ours. And, no matter whether they belong to the higher group as human beings or to the lower group, the animals, all beings primarily seek peace, comfort and security. Life is as dear to a mute creature as it is to a man. Just as one wants happiness and fears pain, just as one wants to live and not to die, so do other creatures.

Cardinal Hinsley (1865-1943)

Cruelty to animals is the degrading attitude of paganism.

John Holmes

A dog is not 'almost human' and I know of no greater insult to the canine race than to describe it as such.

His Holiness the XIV Dalai Lama of Tibet (Born 1935)

Life is as dear to the mute creature as it is to a man. Just as one wants happiness and fears pain, just as one wants to live and not die, so do other creatures.

The Holy Quran, 6:38 (Islam)

There is not an animal [that lives] on the earth, Nor a being that flies on its wings, but [forms part of] communities like you. Nothing have we omitted from the Book, and they all shall all be gathered to their lord in the end.

Eric Hoffer (1902-1983), American Philosopher

Compassion alone stands apart from the continuous traffic between good and evil proceeding within us. Compassion is the anti-toxin of the soul.

Frank Hoffman, Retired Businessman and Church Pastor

Let no animal suffer or die that we may live!

Frank Hoffman, Retired Businessman and Church Pastor: (In answer to an email question 3 Jan 2013)

> When people accuse us of preaching outside the church, we usually tell them we're not preaching; we're only telling you the truth on behalf of the animals who cannot speak for themselves, because your lifestyle is causing them immense pain and suffering, and they want you to stop.

Frank Hoffman, Retired Businessman and Church Pastor: (Sermon of 9 Sep. 2012)

> Peace-making is a work of love and compassion. It is never passive. It is always active, and seeks to end our warring madness against all humans and other animals, and all other forms of violence.

Frank Hoffman, Retired Businessman and Church Pastor

> The raising and killing of animals for food is the greatest atrocity that the world has ever known, and the greatest spiritual and physical plague upon the human race. The only cure is to live a vegan lifestyle, and work to change the world in that direction through every peaceful means we can.

Frank Hoffman, Retired Businessman and Church Pastor

> A person who wears fur gives the impression that they lack empathy for the animals that suffered and died to provide for their lustful desire, and shows that at heart they are really selfish. Even the wearing of faux or fake fur imparts the same impression.

Frank Hoffman, Retired Businessman and Church Pastor

When one group of people holds such power over another, there can be no justice. And there is no love or justice when we use our position to demoralize someone less fortunate than ourselves. ~Sermon (4 Feb 1990)

Frank Hoffman, Retired Businessman and Church Pastor

Salvation is more than saying a sinner's prayer, and saying that one believes, for 'the demons also believe, and shudder' (James 2:19). The evidence of salvation is seen in a changed heart and a loving and compassionate soul that seeks to end the suffering of all humans and animals. Such a person is truly a peace-making child of God (Matthew 5:9).

Frank Hoffman, Retired Businessman and Church Pastor

Fretting about something also makes us tired; thus we spend even less time doing what we could and should be doing.

Frank Hoffman, Retired Businessman and Church Pastor

The simplest answer to, how does the perfection of a saint come to life in Christians of today, is through strong faith in God and living as a loving, compassionate, peace-making child of God toward the whole of God's creation (humans, other animals, and the environment). You set the proper example of kingdom living no matter what others do around you.

Frank Hoffman, Retired Businessman and Church Pastor: About our Foundation and Internet Ministry (2005)

After years in church ministry, we came to the hard conclusion that most churches are morally bankrupt when it comes to being loving and compassionate peacemakers for the whole of creation, especially when it comes to kindness to the animals outside of our own families. Additionally, we had first-hand evidence that cruelty and violence toward animals leads to cruelty and violence toward humans. We wanted to find a way of reaching out to the world around us and shine the light of the Prince of Peace into the dark areas of our society.

Frank Hoffman, Retired Businessman and Church Pastor

If we see the temporary success of evildoers, and become envious of them for what they have, then we are apt to do as they do, which isn't very wise.

Mary Hoffman

In my opinion, most research utilizing animals is merely subsidized sadism masquerading as 'science'.

Mary Hoffman

It appears that much of today's Christianity has been hijacked by the hard-hearted, who have their own agenda, and lead others to share their eternal misery. This form of Christianity has no resemblance to the teachings of Jesus Christ, as reflected in the Sermon on the Mount.

Oliver Wendell Holmes (1902-1932), U.S. Supreme Court Associate Justice

Controversy equalizes fools and wise men - and the fools know it.

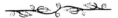

Clementine Homilies (2nd Century AD)

The unnatural eating of flesh-meats is as polluting as the heathen worship of devils, with its sacrifices and its impure feasts, through participation in which a man becomes a fellow-eater with devils.

Victor Hugo (1802-1885), French Poet, Novelist, Playwright and Essayist

First it was necessary to civilize man in relation to man. Now it is necessary to civilize man in relation to nature and the animals.

Victor Hugo (1802-1885), French Poet, Novelist, Playwright and Essayist

I believe that pity is a law like justice, and that kindness is a duty like uprightness.

Aldous Huxley (1894-1963), Author

Compared with that of Taoists and Far Eastern Buddhists, the Christian attitude toward Nature has been curiously insensitive and often downright domineering and violent. Taking their cue from an unfortunate remark in Genesis, Catholic moralists have regarded animals as mere things which men do right to regard for their own ends....

Aldous Huxley (1894-1963), Author

To his dog, every man is Napoleon; hence the constant popularity of dogs.

Reverend William Ralph Inge (1860-1854), Anglican Priest, Professor of Divinity, Oxford University, UK

We have enslaved the rest of the animal creation and have treated our distant cousins in fur and feathers so badly that beyond doubt, if they were able to formulate a religion, they would depict the Devil in human form.

Reverend William Ralph Inge (1860-1854), Anglican Priest, Professor of Divinity, Oxford University, UK

The great discovery of the nineteenth century, that we are of one blood with the lower animals, has created new ethical obligations which have not yet penetrated the public conscience. The clerical profession has been lamentably remiss in preaching this obvious duty.

Henrik Ibsen

It is inexcusable for scientists to torture animals; let them make their experiments on journalists and politicians.

Reverend William Ralph Inge (1860-1854), Anglican Priest, Professor of Divinity, Oxford University, UK

Deliberate cruelty to our defenceless and beautiful little cousins is surely one of the meanest and most detestable vices of which a human being can be guilty.

Reverend William Ralph Inge (1860-1854), Anglican Priest, Professor of Divinity, Oxford University, UK

A cat can be trusted to purr when she is pleased, which is more than can be said for human beings.

Irenaeus of Lyons, Bishop of Lugdunum in Gaul, now Lyons, France (130- 202AD): The Ante-Nicene Fathers, Vol. I, reprinted 1977, (P512)

But the law of liberty, that is, the word of God, preached by the apostles (who went forth from Jerusalem) throughout all the earth, caused such a change in the state of things, that these [nations] did form the swords and war-lances into ploughshares, and changed them into pruning-hooks for reaping the corn, [that is], into instruments used for peaceful purposes, and that they are now unaccustomed to fighting, but when smitten, offer also the other cheek.

Isaiah 11:6-9

The wolf also shall dwell with the lamb,
And the leopard shall lie down with the kid,
And a little child shall lead them...
They shall not hurt nor destroy in all my holy mountain.
For the earth shall be full of the knowledge of the Lord,
As the waters cover the sea.

Holbrook Jackson

Man is a dog's idea of what God should be. [Tragically, their trust is often mistaken and they are let down by humanity.]

Anna Jameson (1794-1860), Dublin-born, Irish Writer on Art: Winter Studies and Summer Rambles

The true purpose of education is to cherish and unfold the seed of immortality already sown within us; to develop, to their fullest extent, the capacities of every kind with which the God who made us has endowed us.

Jainism

Ahimsa-paramo-dharmah - Non-injury to living beings is the highest religion.

Anna Jameson (1794-1860), Dublin-born, Irish Writer on Art

I do not remember ever to have heard the kind and just treatment of animals enforced on Christian principles or made the subject of a sermon.

Thomas Jefferson (1743-1826), The 3rd President of the USA

I tremble for my species when I reflect that God is just.

Judith Jenya, Runs Summer Camps for 'Disadvantaged' Children in Bosnia: From Modern Maturity, (Nov-Dec 2000)

I believe that bullies can only bully if they smell fear. They don't have a clue what to do with strength and truth.

Edward Jesse

With the exception of women, there is nothing on earth as agreeable or necessary to the comfort of man as the dog.

Jesus (3 AD-36AD): Extract from the Essene Gospel of Peace
And the flesh of slain beasts in his body will become his own tomb. For I tell you truly, he who kills kills himself and whoso eats the flesh of slain beast eats the body of death.

Job 12: 7-10 (Judaism and Christianity)

You have only to ask the cattle, for them to instruct you, and the birds of the sky, for them to inform you. The creeping things of earth will give you lessons, and the fish of the sea provide you an explanation: there is not one such creature but will know that the hand of God has arranged things like this! In his hand is the soul of every living thing and the breath of every human being!

Samuel Johnson (1709-1784), English Writer

Great works are performed, not by strength, but by perseverance.

Sir William Jones (1746-1794), English Philologist, Jurist and Poet

Cruelty to dumb [unspeaking] animals is one of the distinguishing vices of the low and base minded. Wherever it is found, it is a certain mark of ignorance and meanness; a mark which all the external advantages of wealth, splendour and nobility cannot obliterate. It is consistent neither with learning nor true civility.

Franklin P. Jones

Scratch a dog and you'll find a permanent job.

Carl Jung (1905-1961), Swiss Psychiatrist

During my medical education at the University of Basel, I found vivisection horrible, barbarous, and above all, unnecessary.

David Starr Jordan (1851-1931), MD, Educator, Scientist and Peace Activist. An expert in many fields, he was President of Indiana University and later President of Stanford University.

When a dog barks at the moon, then it is religion; but when he barks at strangers, it is patriotism!

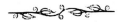

Franz Kafka (1883-1924), Famous Austrian-Czech Writer. (Remark made whilst sympathizing with a fish in an aquarium.)

Now I can look at you in peace; I don't eat you anymore.

David Starr Jordan (1851-1931), MD, Educator, Scientist and Peace Activist. An expert in many fields, he was President of Indiana University and later President of Stanford University.

Be a life long or short, its completeness depends on what it was lived for.

David Starr Jordan (1851-1931), MD, Educator, Scientist and Peace Activist. An expert in many fields, he was President of Indiana University and later President of Stanford University.

Our treatment of animals will someday be considered barbarous. There cannot be perfect civilization until man realizes that the rights of every living creature are as sacred as his own.

Immanuel Kant (1724–1804), German Philosopher

Parents usually educate their children merely in such a manner that however bad the world may be, they may adapt themselves to its present conditions. But they ought to give them an education so much better than this, that a better condition of things may thereby be brought about in the future.

Immanuel Kant (1724–1804), German Philosopher

...We can judge the heart of a man by his treatment of animals.

Casey Kasem, American Top 40 Radio Personality

My favorite quote says it all: 'Become a vegan/vegetarian: your body will respect you for your wisdom and the animals will love you for your compassion.'

Stephen R. Kaufman, Physician and Author

From a Christian perspective, all Creation belongs to God. Mistreating any part of Creation shows disrespect for God. The growing ecological crisis, increasing human poverty, and widespread animal abuse all relate to humans putting desires of the flesh before our obligations to serve God.

Thomas Kempis (1379-1471)

And if thy heart be straight with God, then every creature shall be to thee a mirror of life and a book of holy doctrine, for there is no creature so little or so vile, but that sheweth and representeth the goodness of God

John Harvey Kellogg (1852-1943), American Surgeon & Founder of Battle Creek Sanatorium

Flesh foods are not the best nourishment for human beings and were not the food of our primitive ancestors. They are secondary or second-hand products, since all food comes originally from the vegetable kingdom. There is nothing necessary or desirable for human nutrition to be found in meats or flesh foods which is not found in and derived from vegetable products. A dead cow or sheep lying in a pasture is recognized as carrion. The same sort of carcass dressed and hung up in a butcher's stall passes as food! Careful microscopic examination may show little or no difference between the fence corner carcass and the butcher shop carcass. Both are swarming with colon germs and redolent with putrefaction.

William Kellogg (1860-1951)

How can you eat anything with eyes?

Martin Luther King, Jr. (1929-1968), Reverend and US Civil Leader

The ultimate weakness of violence is that it is a descending spiral, begetting the very thing it seeks to destroy. Instead of diminishing evil, it multiplies it... Through violence you may murder the hater, but you do not murder hate. In fact, violence merely increases hate...Returning violence for violence multiplies violence, adding deeper darkness to a night already devoid of stars. Darkness cannot drive out hate; only love can do that.

Soren Kierkegaard, Christian Theologian: Christian Discourses, trans. Walter Lowie, Oxford: Oxford University Press, 1940, (P322)

If thou art absolutely obedient to God, then there is no ambiguity in thee and... thou art mere simplicity before God.... One thing there is which all Satan's cunning and all the snares of temptation cannot take by surprise and that is simplicity.

Martin Luther King, Jr. (1929-1968), Reverend and US Civil Leader

Never be afraid to do what's right, especially if the well-being of a person or animal is at stake. Society's punishments are small compared to the wounds we inflict on our soul when we look the other way.

Michael Klaper, M.D. American Author, Physician and International Lecturer

I know a lot of people are on a continuum, evolving their diet from red meat to chicken, to fish, and to dairy products - finally evolving to a vegan diet, completely free of animal products. If you are on this continuum - if you are moving towards a pure vegetarian diet, I urge you not to linger in 'chicken-and-fish land' too long. Besides having large amounts of concentrated protein, which can leach calcium from the bones, today's fish is by far the most polluted of all the flesh foods. Fish flesh regularly contains toxic chemical pollutants known to cause cancer, kidney failure, nerve damage and birth defects. For this reason, I really feel that fish does not offer much at all in the way of a health food, and if it's the last vestige of animal products remaining in your diet, have no compunction about letting it swim off your plate altogether.

Michael Klaper, M.D. American Author, Physician and International Lecturer

People are the only animals that drink the milk of the mother of another species. All other animals stop drinking milk altogether after weaning. It is unnatural for a dog to nurse from a mother giraffe; it is just as unnatural for a human being to drink the milk of a cow.

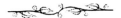

Michael Klaper, M.D. American Author, Physician and International Lecturer

My single greatest challenge is to remain centred and loving in an overwhelmingly non vegan world. In today's world, cruelty and exploitation of other beings - human and nonhuman alike - are accepted, practiced, and profited from by most every institution of society - from commerce and science to education and entertainment. Unfortunately, the vast majority of Homo sapiens are either unaware of the cruelty or accept it as unavoidable and even normal.

Michael Klaper, M.D. American Author, Physician and International Lecturer

The very saddest sound in all my memory was burned into my awareness at age five on my uncle's dairy farm in Wisconsin. A cow had given birth to a beautiful male calf... On the second day after birth, my uncle took the calf from the mother and placed him in the veal pen in the barn - only ten yards away, in plain view of his mother. The mother cow could see her infant, smell him, hear him, but could not touch him, comfort him, or nurse him. The heartrending bellows that she poured forth - minute after minute, hour after hour, for five long days - were excruciating to listen to. They are the most poignant and painful auditory memories I carry in my brain. [The calf would have finally been taken away for slaughter.]

95

Michael Klaper, M.D. American Author, Physician and International Lecturer

All red meat contains saturated fat. There is no such thing as truly lean meat. Trimming away the edge ring of fat around a steak really does not lower the fat content significantly. People who have red meat (trimmed or untrimmed) as a regular feature of their diets suffer in far greater numbers from heart attacks and strokes.

Michael Klaper, M.D. American Author, Physician and International Lecturer

The human body has no more need for cows' milk than it does for dogs' milk, horses' milk, or giraffes' milk!!

Michael Klaper, M.D. American Author, Physician and International Lecturer: From: Incredibly Delicious: Gentle World, (P14)

Every nutrient we require – proteins, vitamins, minerals and others – can be obtained (or synthesized by the human body) from plant-based foods.

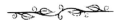

Michael Klaper, M.D. American Author, Physician and International Lecturer

The meat-laden, Western style diet, rather than leading us to an age of prosperity and health, has contributed to an epidemic of degenerative diseases. The nations who consume the most meats suffer the highest rates of death from heart attacks, strokes, cancer and diabetes.

Julie Klotter, Medical Doctor: Townsend Medical Letter, May 1995

In reality, cow's milk, especially processed cow's milk, has been linked to a variety of health problems, including: mucous production, haemoglobin loss, childhood diabetes, heart disease, atherosclerosis, arthritis, kidney stones, mood swings, depression, irritability, and allergies.

C. Everett Koop, Former Surgeon General (USA)

Your choice of diet can influence your long term health prospects more than any other action you might take.

Joseph Wood Krutch

When a man wantonly destroys one of the works of man we call him a vandal. When he destroys one of the works of god we call him a sportsman.

Dennis Kucinich, U. S. Congressman and Presidential Candidate: Animal Rights 2003 Conference, August 2003

...Our presence on this planet has a higher calling. That we can through our activism, make light in this world, that we can through our activism, lift up the cause of the humblest beings, that we can through our activism, open up not only our own hearts, but the hearts of people everywhere so that our society can become more compassionate, so that our society can be more loving, so that our society can create policies which are caring for animals.

Milan Kundera ~ Milan Kundera: The Unbearable Lightness of Being: From Eternal Treblinka (P1)

> True human goodness, in all its purity and freedom, can come to the fore only when its recipient has no power. Mankind's true moral test, its fundamental test (which lies deeply from view), consists of its attitude towards those who are at its mercy: animals. And in this respect mankind has suffered a fundamental debacle, a debacle so fundamental that all others stem from it.

Milan Kundera

> To sit with a dog on a hillside on a glorious afternoon is to be back in Eden, where doing nothing was not boring - it was peace.

Lance Landall, New Zealand Poet

Show me a man who can slit a creature's throat as unemotionally as he would slice a tomato, and I'll show you a man whose savaged sensibilities are fertile ground for murderous intent to grow.

Lance Landall, New Zealand Poet

Those who love hunting, must love weapons, and thereby, effectively violence. Where there's no need, it is plain desire, and such perverted desire is by its very nature less respecting of life. When it comes to creatures, man has gone from being their care-taker to being their life-taker. Given that killing creatures is only one step away from killing humans, is it any wonder that man regularly kills his own kind now. I have to ask, who would want to be only one step away?

Lance Landall, New Zealand Poet

It seems rather bizarre to me, and somewhat Jekyll and Hyde, to be sitting at your table devouring a creature while at the same time lovingly stroking another as your pet. But then again, when one's raised that way, I guess the irony (some would say hypocrisy) isn't so easily seen.

Lance Landall, New Zealand Poet

I would rather stroke, cuddle, pamper and protect a creature, than slit, shoot, pluck, skin, gut, stuff, and eat one.

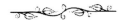

Lance Landall, New Zealand Poet

Creatures eating creatures, and humans doing likewise (they being creatures too), is a tragic practice in a tragic world. A violent and bloody affair. Even within the animal kingdom there are animals that do not eat flesh-food; for example: Elephants, deer, zebras, cows, sheep, etc. This would suggest that a flesh-food diet is not a natural one, but rather a distortion that has occurred at some point, and overtime, regarding those creatures that do.

It also suggests that just as it is not normal (a self-inflicted distortion) for humans to eat flesh-food (given they're clearly herbivores by design) neither is it normal for any creature, and that originally all would have eaten a non-flesh diet. If humans and certain creatures (but a few mentioned) can survive on a plant based diet, I see no reason why all creatures couldn't have at some time. In my mind, there is no doubt that they all did, and that something went amiss. Personally, I would rather not be amiss.

Lance Landall, New Zealand Poet

Going by the biblical record, the original diet for humans was a vegan one. Therefore, if a Christian truly desires to be in harmony with their Creator's intensions, they will remove flesh-food from their diet, and as a consequence will not only avoid the injurious properties of flesh-food, but will also develop a more human nature.

Lance Landall, New Zealand Poet

There's not a doubt in my mind that a lust for killing creatures is an illness.

Lance Landall, New Zealand Poet

The trouble with eating flesh-food is that it only takes one morsel to have something very injurious enter your body that can affect you for many years, and possibly for the rest of your life.

K. D. Lang

We all love animals. Why do we call some 'pets' and others dinner?

K. D. Lang

If you knew how meat was made, you'd probably lose your lunch.

Stanislaw Lec

Each snowflake in an avalanche pleads not guilty.

William Edward Hartpole Lecky (1838-1903)

I venture to maintain that there are multitudes to whom the necessity of discharging the duties of a butcher would be so inexpressibly painful and revolting, that if they could obtain a flesh diet on no other condition, they would relinquish it forever.

William Edward Hartpole Lecky (1838-1903)

The animal world being altogether external to the scheme of redemption, was regarded as beyond the range of duty, and the belief that we have any kind of obligation to its members has never been inculcated - has never, I believe, been even admitted - by Catholic theologians.

William Edward Hartpole Lecky (1838-1903)

Spain and southern Italy, in which Catholicism has most deeply implanted its roots, are even now, probably beyond all other countries in Europe, those in which inhumanity to animals is most wanton and unrebuked.

Aldo Leopold, Conservationist, Forester, Philosopher, Educator, Writer and Outdoor Enthusiast

Only the mountain has lived long enough to listen objectively to the howl of the wolf.

Aldo Leopold, Conservationist, Forester, Philosopher, Educator, Writer and Outdoor Enthusiast

Examine each question in terms of what is ethically and aesthetically right, as well as what is economically expedient. A thing is right when it tends to preserve the integrity, stability, and beauty of the biotic community. It is wrong when it tends otherwise.

Aldo Leopold, Conservationist, Forester, Philosopher, Educator, Writer and Outdoor Enthusiast

Nonconformity is the highest evolutionary attainment of social animals.

Aldo Leopold, Conservationist, Forester, Philosopher, Educator, Writer and Outdoor Enthusiast

Man always kills the thing he loves, and so we the pioneers have killed our wilderness. Some say we had to. Be that as it may, I am glad I shall never be young without wild country to be young in. Of what avail are forty freedoms without a blank spot on the map?

Aldo Leopold, Conservationist, Forester, Philosopher, Educator, Writer and Outdoor Enthusiast

There are some who can live without wild things and some who cannot.

Aldo Leopold, Conservationist, Forester, Philosopher, Educator, Writer and Outdoor Enthusiast

The last word in ignorance is the man who says of an animal or plant: 'What good is it?

C.S. Lewis, Author

If we cut up beasts simply because they cannot prevent us and because we are backing our own side in the struggle for existence, it is only logical to cut up imbeciles, criminals, enemies, or capitalists for the same reasons.

Dr. Harry Lillie: Dr. Harry Lillie, 1975

That night in my sleeping bag on the floor of the cabin, I dreamed a big beaver was climbing gently on to my jacket pillow. It woke me and I felt something moving at my hair, then retreating to the floor. In the beam of my torch, there was a little White Footed mouse; and in her mouth a great faggot of what looked suspiciously like my hair.
She scampered off to where an old broken piece of armchair lay in a corner. I waited in the dark and she was back almost at once and up at my head, her tiny pink hands and teeth cutting the required lengths for that nest. I went to sleep again thinking it was so nice to know that man, the only true pest in Nature, was at last of some use to at least one little person in that vast wilderness.

C.S. Lewis, Author

Pain insists upon being attended to. God whispers to us in our pleasures, speaks in our consciences, but shouts in our pains. It is his megaphone to rouse a deaf world.

Abraham Lincoln (1809-1865), President of the United States: (Reply to friends who chided him for delaying them by stopping to return a fledgling to its nest.)

I could not have slept to-night if I had left that helpless little creature to perish on the ground.

Abraham Lincoln (1809-1865), President of the United States

Nearly all men can stand adversity, but if you want to test a man's [or woman's] character, give him [or her] power.

Abraham Lincoln (1809-1865), President of the United States

To sin by silence when they should protest makes cowards of men.

Abraham Lincoln (1809-1865), President of the United States

You cannot escape the responsibility of tomorrow by evading it today.

Abraham Lincoln (1809-1865), President of the United States

America will never be destroyed from the outside. If we falter and lose our freedoms, it will be because we destroyed ourselves.

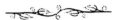

Abraham Lincoln (1809-1865), President of the United States

Don't pray that God's on our side pray that we're on his side.

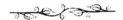

Abraham Lincoln (1809-1865), President of the United States

I am a firm believer in the people. If given the truth, they can be depended upon to meet any national crises. The great point is to bring them the real facts.

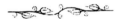

Abraham Lincoln (1809-1865), President of the United States

Force is all-conquering, but its victories are short-lived.

Abraham Lincoln (1809-1865), President of the United States

I have always found that mercy bears richer fruits than strict justice.

Abraham Lincoln (1809-1865), President of the United States

Character is like a tree and reputation like its shadow. The shadow is what we think of it; the tree is the real thing.

Abraham Lincoln (1809-1865), President of the United States

It often requires more courage to dare to do right than to fear to do wrong.

Abraham Lincoln (1809-1865), President of the United States

Most folks are about as happy as they make up their minds to be.

Abraham Lincoln (1809-1865), President of the United States

No man is good enough to govern another man without that other's consent.

Abraham Lincoln (1809-1865), President of the United States

The ballot is stronger than the bullet.

Abraham Lincoln (1809-1865), President of the United States

The probability that we may fail in the struggle ought not to deter us from the support of a cause we believe to be just.

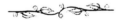

Abraham Lincoln (1809-1865), President of the United States

Those who would deny freedom to others deserve it not for themselves; and, under a just God, cannot long retain it.

Abraham Lincoln (1809-1865), President of the United States

You may deceive all the people part of the time, and part of the people all the time, but not all the people all the time.

Abraham Lincoln (1809-1865), President of the United States

We live in the midst of alarms; anxiety beclouds the future; we expect some new disaster with each newspaper we read.

Abraham Lincoln (1809-1865), President of the United States

There's no honorable way to kill, no gentle way to destroy.

Abraham Lincoln (1809-1865), President of the United States

Our defense is in the preservation of the spirit which prizes liberty as a heritage of all men, in all lands, everywhere. Destroy this spirit and you have planted the seeds of despotism around your own doors.

Abraham Lincoln (1809-1865), President of the United States

The philosophy of the school room in one generation will be the philosophy of government in the next.

Abraham Lincoln (1809-1865), President of the United States

My dream is of a place and a time where America will once again be seen as the last best hope of earth.

Charles A. Lindbergh (1902-1974)

In wilderness I sense the miracle of life, and behind it our scientific accomplishments fade to trivia.

The Author, Reverend Andrew Linzey

Justice requires a thoroughgoing revision of our treatment of animals (and) historical theology creatively expounded also requires this.

Carolus Linnaeus (1707-1778) Medical Doctor and Botanist: Introduced binomial nomenclature (Naming plants and animals according to their physical structure)

Man's structure, external and internal, compared with that of other animals shows that fruit and succulent vegetables constitute his natural food.

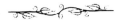

Henry Wadsworth Longfellow (1807-1882) American Poet

Being all fashioned of the same dust,
Let us be merciful as well as just.

The Author, Reverend Andrew Linzey: From Christianity and the Rights of Animals, 1988

Since an animal's natural life is a gift from God, it follows that God's right is violated when the natural life of his creatures is perverted. Those who, in contrast, opt for the welfarist approach to intensive farming are inevitably involved in speculating how far such and such may or may not suffer in what are plainly unnatural conditions. But unless animals are judged to have some right to their natural life, from what standpoint can we judge abnormalities, mutilations or adjustments? Confining a de-beaked hen in a battery cage is more than a moral crime; it is a living sign of our failure to recognize the blessing of God in creation.

John Locke (1632-1704), English Philosopher

New opinions are always suspected and usually opposed, without any other reason, but because they are not already common.

Henry Wadsworth Longfellow (1807-1882), American Poet

How can I teach your children gentleness and mercy to the weak, and reverence for life, which in its nakedness and excess, is still a gleam of God's omnipotence, when by your laws, your actions and your speech, you contradict the very things I teach?

Henry Wadsworth Longfellow (1807-1882) American Poet

All things must change to something new.

The Author, Reverend Andrew Linzey

To stand for Christ is to stand against the evil of cruelty inflicted on those who are weak, vulnerable, unprotected, undefended, morally innocent and in that class we must unambiguously include animals.

Henry Wadsworth Longfellow (1807-1882) American Poet

Among the noblest in the land –
though man may count himself the least –
That man I honor and revere,
Who without favor, without fear,
In the great city dares to stand,
The friend of every friendless beast.

Konrad Lorenz

There is no faith which has never yet been broken, except that of a truly faithful dog.

Howard Lyman, Ex-Cattle Rancher turned Vegan, International Lecturer, Founder of the non-profit: Voice for a Viable Future and Author of the Best-Selling book: Mad Cowboy. His Mad Cowboy Documentary is a DVD also shown on TV.

To consider yourself an environmentalist and still eat meat is like saying you're a philanthropist who doesn't give to charity.

Howard Lyman, Ex-Cattle Rancher turned Vegan, International Lecturer, Founder of the non-profit: Voice for a Viable Future and Author of the Best-Selling book: Mad Cowboy. His Mad Cowboy Documentary is a DVD also shown on TV.

> Family farmers are victims of public policy that gives preference to feeding animals over feeding people. This has encouraged the cheap grain policy of this nation and has made the beef cartel the biggest hog at the trough.

Howard Lyman, Ex-Cattle Rancher turned Vegan, International Lecturer, Founder of the non-profit: Voice for a Viable Future and Author of the Best-Selling book: Mad Cowboy. His Mad Cowboy Documentary is a DVD also shown on TV.

> I believe if the viewing of slaughter was required to eat meat, most folks would become vegetarians.

Howard Lyman, Ex-Cattle Rancher turned Vegan, International Lecturer, Founder of the non-profit: Voice for a Viable Future and Author of the Best-Selling book: Mad Cowboy. His Mad Cowboy Documentary is a DVD also shown on TV.

> Running the ranch paid well; it was challenging; it was my family tradition. But my conscience told me that I needed to speak out about this industry - there's just too much that the cattle industry hides from the public.

Howard Lyman, Ex-Cattle Rancher turned Vegan, International Lecturer, Founder of the non-profit: Voice for a Viable Future and Author of the Best-Selling book: Mad Cowboy. His Mad Cowboy Documentary is a DVD also shown on TV.

Veganism isn't just a strict vegetarian diet; it is a complete philosophical viewpoint. It is practical in outlook, simple to understand and aspires to the highest environmental and spiritual values. I am sure it holds the key to a future lifestyle for a humane planetary guardianship...

J.H.C. Tabucur Lyrette

Negative Karma is a black cloud in excess it hides the light of enlightenment. Zero karma, is positive karma. Save a life, not take one.

J.H.C. Tabucur Lyrette

We speak for those, you cannot hear!

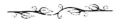

J.H.C. Tabucur Lyrette

Our planet is shrouded in bad karma, due to human activity, we kill man en-mass, we kill the animals, soil, water and air, which has an overall negative effect on the earth and on our own spiritual evolution. When we free ourselves of karma, we free our planet from karma. Yin and yang, in perfect harmony. This is the natural way of things, the way of nature, that which we call the Tao (Dao), the Way.

J.H.C. Tabucur Lyrette

Non-Vegans kill well over several hundreds of billion animals (chickens, cows, pigs, sheep and goats, fish, etc...) annually. Breaking the law ('Thou Shall Not Kill'). These activities prevent man from achieving 'Global Enlightenment' (Sham-b-hala-Bud-dh-ist/Kal-ki of Sambhala-H--indu). Or in other words, Heaven on Earth.

J.H.C Tabucur Lyrette

How is it we know that they wish to live, for the same reason we all wish to live, to be, to exist. That is the driving force of life itself, to flourish, to enjoy the physical realm, this universe, for the brief moments we all have. The Milky Way takes 250 million years to revolve once, how much time do we all have, and to rob others of that experience, how selfish?

J.H.C. Tabucur Lyrette

If all humans knew that killing, and consuming flesh, would deny them entrance to heaven, who among you would eat flesh? Nirvana can be obtained in a lifetime or a few, depending on your karma (your past), and how you live in your present life. Or in multiple lifetimes (-hundreds-), the choice is yours.

J.H.C. Tabucur Lyrette

Cattle and all live stock are born to hell in our world, yet we selectively choose, who to be humane to, like our pets we love so dearly. It's a shame you cannot find it in your hearts to extend that love to other higher life forms. Ever met a Cow, good folks, [she would] would never do you wrong?

J.H.C Tabucur Lyrette

And what gives us the right to kill others who evolved and share this world with us. In my heart they are my brothers & sisters, and it is our universal duty to preserve life. My soul screams when I hear them plead as best as they can for their lives to be spared, for only their words to fall on your deaf ears, to you they have no voice, to us they speak volumes.

Count Maurice Maeterlinck (1862-1949)

Were the belief one day to become general that man could dispense with animal food, there would ensue not only a great economic revolution, but a moral improvement as well.

Wangari Maathai, Nobel-Prize Winner, Founder of Kenya's Greenbelt Movement

There is a terrible forest fire. All the animals are fleeing the conflagration except for a Hummingbird, who is flying back and forth, scooping up little slivers of water from a spring and dumping them on the flames. 'What do you think you're doing, stupid little bird?' the other animals ask derisively, and Hummingbird says, 'I'm doing what I can.'

George MacDonald (1824-1905), Minister, Poet and Novelist

To be trusted is a greater compliment than to be loved.

Count Maurice Maeterlinck (1862-1949)

In the world which we know, among the different and primitive geniuses that preside over the evolution of the several species, there exists not one, excepting that of the dog that ever gave a thought to the presence of man.

George MacDonald (1824–1905), Minister, Poet and ovelist

We are often unable to tell people what they need to know because they want to know something else.

Paul and Linda McCartney: Animal Rights Activists

If slaughterhouses had glass walls, everyone would be a vegetarian. We feel better about ourselves and better about the animals, knowing we're not contributing to their pain.

George MacDonald (1824-1905), Minister, Poet and Novelist (The Fantastic Imagination)

The best thing you can do for your fellow, next to rousing his conscience, is not to give him things to think about, but to wake things up that are in him; or say, to make him think things for himself.

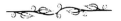

Rue McClanahan, Actress

Compassion is the foundation of everything positive, everything good. If you carry the power of compassion to the marketplace and the dinner table, you can make your life really count.

Paul and Linda McCartney: Animal Rights Activists

We stopped eating meat many years ago. During the course of a Sunday lunch we happened to look out of the kitchen window at our young lambs playing happily in the fields. Glancing down at our plates, we suddenly realized that we were eating the leg of an animal who had until recently been playing in a field herself. We looked at each other and said, "Wait a minute, we love these sheep - they're such gentle creatures. So why are we eating them?" It was the last time we ever did.

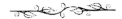

James McWilliams

When hens are owned by humans to produce a good for human use, they will never be treated with the dignity that they deserve. More to the point, they will almost always be stripped of all dignity so we can waste their bodily by-products on a holiday ritual that asks us to take a bunny hiding eggs seriously enough to kill untold numbers of real chickens.

James Marcus

Some say vegetarianism is an alternative diet, but it is the original diet, the plan designed by God.

John McDougall, MD

Open heart-surgery is radical. Eating oatmeal and potatoes is not radical.

Rue McClanahan, Actress

Fur used to turn heads, now it turns stomachs.

Frederic Addison McGrand (1895-1988), Physician, Politician, Humanitarian and Founder of the Canadian Humane Societies

Cruelty has cursed the human family for countless ages. It is almost impossible for one to be cruel to animals and kind to humans. If children are permitted to be cruel to their pets and other animals, they easily learn to get the same pleasure from the misery of fellow-humans. Such tendencies can easily lead to crime.

Charles R. Magel, Professor

Ask the experimenters why they experiment on animals, and the answer is: 'Because the animals are like us.' Ask the experimenters why it is morally okay to experiment on animals, and the answer is: ' Because the animals are not like us.' Animal experimentation rests on a logical contradiction.

Justin Martyr (100-165 AD), Catholic Saint: Dialogue with Trypho 110.3. Written by St. Justin about 160 AD

We ourselves were well conversant with war, murder, and everything evil, but all of us throughout the whole wide earth have traded in our weapons of war. We have exchanged our swords for ploughshares, our spears for farm tools. Now we cultivate the fear of God, justice, kindness to men, faith, and the expectation of the future given to us by the Father himself through the Crucified One.

Jim Mason, Author

Animals have been regarded as property for way too long. It's high time we took on a more loving and responsible relationship with our kindred beings in the web of life on this beautiful planet. I always think and act as a guardian towards my kindred beings, never as their owner.

Jim Mason, Author

Americans, at least, have a tremendous appetite for meat, dairy products and eggs. They have little appetite, however, for information on the lives of the animals that produce what they eat. Perhaps they sense something. Do they sense that beyond the mountain of steaks, hamburgers, sausages, cold cuts, ice cream, milkshakes, cheeses, pizzas, pastries, soufflés and omelets consumed each year lies a whole mountain range of animal suffering and death?

James Michener (1902-1997), American Author and Novelist: Where Did the Animals Go? Readers' Digest, June 1976

...Every animal that walks the earth, or swims or flies is precious beyond description, something so rare and wonderful that it equals the stars or the ocean or the mind of man...

Edwin Markham (1852-1940), American Poet and Lecturer

We have committed the golden rule to memory; let us now commit it to life.

Jim Mason, Author

It is the worldview of the human supremacist: The view or belief held by one species, Homo sapiens sapiens, that it has a divine right - a God-given license - to use animals and everything else in the living world for its own benefit. This worldview is strongest in Western traditions, but it has spread to Russia, China, Japan and most of the rest of the world.

Vesanto Melina

To the greatest extent possible, I try to make choices that involve the least amount of cruelty and environmental damage. I'm interested in sustainable agriculture, environmental issues, human rights, and my interconnectedness in the web of life. It is a great pleasure for me to find products and practices that have a positive effect on living beings and the environment, rather than a negative one.

Jim Mason, Author

Some think human society seems to be steadily going insane. They note the ridiculous hatreds that keep us nearly constantly at war with each other. They see we are fouling our global nest, wiping out much of the planet's life and making life more and more miserable for ourselves. I don't think we are going insane; I think we have just not learned to look deeply enough into the causes of our current social and environmental problems. I believe with a growing number of others that these problems began several millennia ago when our ancestors took up farming and broke the primal bonds with the living world and put human beings above all other life...

Geoffrey Mather (1910-), Clergyman

I write in sorrow [on vivisection]: as far as I can tell, no voice has been heard from the Church about this evil. The matter is forgotten for another year. It should not be. It is one of the most appalling blots on our plentifully blotted civilisation.

Charles Mayo PhD (The Mayo Clinic)

I abhor vivisection. It should at least be curbed. Better, it should be abolished. I know of no achievement through vivisection, no scientific discovery that could not have been obtained without such barbarism and cruelty. The whole thing is evil.

Margaret Mead (1901-1978), American Anthropologist

One of the most dangerous things that can happen to a child is to kill or torture an animal and get away with it.

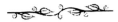

Margaret Mead

Never doubt that a small group of thoughtful, committed, citizens can change the world. Indeed, it is the only thing that ever has.

John Stuart Mill (1806-1873), English Philosopher and Economist

No great improvements in the lot of mankind are possible until a great change takes place in the fundamental constitution of their modes of thought.

Herman Melville (1819-1891), Author

Go to the meat market of a Saturday night and see the crowds of live bipeds staring up at the long rows of dead quadrupeds. Does not that sight take the tooth out of the cannibal's jaw? Cannibals? Who is not a cannibal? I tell you it will be more tolerable for the Fejee that salted down a lean missionary in his cellar against a coming famine; it will be more tolerable for that provident Fejee, I say, in the day of judgement, than for thee, civilized and enlightened gourmand, who nailest geese to the ground and feastest on their bloated livers in thy pate-de-foie-gras.

John Stuart Mill (1806-1873), English Philosopher and Economist

Granted that any practice causes more pain to animals than it give pleasure to man; is that practice moral or immoral? And if, exactly in proportion as human beings raise their heads out of the slough of selfishness, they do not with one voice answer 'Immoral,' let the morality of the principle of utility be forever condemned.

John Stuart Mill (1806-1873), English Philosopher and Economist

One person with a belief is equal to a force of ninety-nine with only interests.

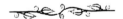

John Stuart Mill (1806-1873), English Philosopher and Economist

The reasons for legal intervention in favor of children apply not less strongly to the case of those unfortunate slaves - the animals.

John Stuart Mill (1806-1873), English Philosopher and Economist

It often happens that the universal belief of one age, a belief from which no one was free or could be free without an extraordinary effort of genius or courage, becomes to a subsequent age, so palpable an absurdity, that the only difficulty is to imagine how such an idea could ever have appeared credible.

Bradley Miller

Teaching a child not to step on a caterpillar is as valuable to the child as it is to the caterpillar.

Thomas Moffett

Men dig their graves with their own teeth and die by those fated instruments more than the weapons of their enemies.

Rev. A.M. Mitchell, M.A., Vicar of Burton Wood, Lancashire, Extract from: The Church and Food Reform: The Herald of the Golden Age, April 1910

Are we to eat just what we like, what we choose, without regard to the pain and suffering, to the rights of the creatures in our power, to the naturalness or unnaturalness of the food they supply, or, again, to the possible physical, mental, and moral injury their flesh may do to those who eat of it?...The animal has its rights, and can claim from us these two - Justice and Mercy.

Moby, Musician

Intellectually, human beings and animals may be different, but it's pretty obvious that animals have a rich emotional life and that they feel joy and pain. It's easy to forget the connection between a hamburger and the cow it came from, but I forced myself to acknowledge the fact that every time I ate a hamburger, a cow had ceased to breathe and moo and walk around.

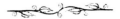

Ashley Montague

The indifference, callousness and contempt that so many people exhibit toward animals is evil first because it results in great suffering in animals, and second because it results in an incalculably great impoverishment of the human spirit. All education should be directed toward the refinement of the individual's sensibilities in relation not only to one's fellow humans everywhere, but to all things whatsoever.

Michel De Montaigne (1533-1592), French Essayist

For my part I have never been able to see, without displeasure, an innocent and defenseless animal, from whom we receive no offense or harm, pursued and slaughtered.

Lynda Montgomery

Why does Sea World have a seafood restaurant? I'm halfway through my fish burger and I realize, Oh my God. I could be eating a slow learner.

Mary Tyler Moore (Born 1936), American Actress

Behind every beautiful fur, there is a story. It is a bloody, barbaric story.

Howard J Moore (1862-1916), Chicago Professor of Zoology

Man is not the pedestalled creature pictured by his imagination - a being glittering with prerogatives, and towering apart from and above all other beings. He is a pain-shunning, pleasure-seeking, death-dreading organism, differing in particulars, but not in kind, from the pain-shunning, pleasure-seeking, death-dreading organisms below and around him.

Sir Thomas More
The utopians feel that slaughtering our fellow creatures gradually destroys the sense of compassion, which is the finest sentiment of which our human nature is capable.

Axel Munthe (1857-1949)

The wild cruel beast is not behind the bars of the cage. He is in front of it.

Sue Murphy

Did you ever walk into a room and forget why you walked in? I think that is how dogs spend their lives.

Rev. Prebendary Moss, Head Master of Shrewsbury School: Extract from: The Gospel of Humanity: The Herald of the Golden Age, March 1900

Thou shalt not muzzle the ox when he treadeth out the corn.
Deuteronomy 4

This is something more than a moral precept; it breathes the spirit of chivalry. It reads like the product of a far later age than that in which it was framed. For, that animals have rights is a modern idea – an idea which even in our own day is recognised only partially and imperfectly. ...why should we invoke, as a justification of our behaviour to animals, a principle on which we should be ashamed to act in relation to human beings?

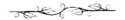

Ingrid Newkirk Founder of PETA (People for the Ethical Treatment of Animals

Recognize meat for what it really is: the antibiotic-and pesticide-laden corpse of a tortured animal.

John G. Neihardt in Black Elk Speaks (American Indian)

Is not the sky a father and the earth a mother, and are not all living things with feet or wings or roots their children? Hear me, four quarters of the world...a relative I am! Give me the strength to walk the soft earth, a relative to all that is, all over the earth, the faces of living things are all alike.

Cardinal John Henry Newman (1801-90), Roman Catholic Cardinal
Cruelty to animals is as if man did not love God...there is something so dreadful, so Satanic, in tormenting those who have never harmed us, and who cannot defend themselves, who are utterly in our power.

Cardinal John Henry Newman (1801-90), Roman Catholic Cardinal

Now what is it moves our very heart and sickens us so much as cruelty shown to poor brutes? I suppose this: first, that they have done us no harm; next, that they have no power whatever of resistance; it is the cowardice and tyranny of which they are the victims which make their sufferings so especially touching... there is something so very dreadful, so satanic, in tormenting those who have never harmed us and who cannot defend themselves; who are utterly in our power.

Cardinal John Henry Newman (1801-90), Roman Catholic Cardinal

To live is to change, and to be perfect is to have changed often.

Cardinal John Henry Newman (1801-90), Roman Catholic Cardinal

It is almost a definition of a gentleman to say he is one who never inflicts pain.

S. D. Newton

I have personally known and dearly loved many of the creatures science calls Rattus rattus a.k.a. Black Rat, Ship Rat, Tree Rat, Roof Rat, etc. That the world so persecutes these clean, charming, intelligent beings is just more evidence of the fallen state of Man.

S. D. Newton

Compassion for our fellow creatures is foundational to the ethical treatment of our own species. It's a bit paradoxical, but the proof is in how badly we treat fellow humans when our consciences have been dulled by disregard for other creatures.

Friedrich Nietzsche (1844-1900), German Philosopher
All ancient philosophy was oriented toward the simplicity of life and taught a certain kind of modesty in one's need. In light of this, the few philosophic vegetarians have done more for mankind than all new philosophers, and as long as philosophers do not take courage to seek out a totally changed way of life and to demonstrate it by their example, they are worth nothing.

Friedrich Nietzsche (1844-1900), German Philosopher
About sacrifice and the offering of sacrifices, sacrificial animals think quite differently from those who look on: but they have never been allowed to have their say.

Vaslav Nijinski (1889-1950), Russian Ballet Dancer and Choreographer

I do not like eating meat because I have seen lambs and pigs killed. I saw and felt their pain. They felt their approaching deaths. I could not bear it. I cried like a child, I ran up a hill and could not breathe. I felt that I was choking. I felt the death of the lamb.

Barack Obama, U.S. Senator, IL - President of the United States

It has not always been the pragmatist, the voice of reason, or the force of compromise, that has created the conditions for liberty, (speaking about the 19th century antislavery movement). Knowing this, I can't summarily dismiss those possessed of similar certainty today - the antiabortion activist ... the animal rights activist who raids a laboratory - no matter how deeply I disagree with their views. I am robbed even of the certainty of uncertainty - for sometimes absolute truths may well be absolute.

Frank A. Oski, Physician: From Incredibly Delicious, Gentle World, (P95)

There's no reason to drink cow's milk at any time in your life. It was designed for calves, not humans, and we should all stop drinking it today.

Kim Ogden-Avrutik, Author: Extract from: Ask the Animals

Why should we believe that we are spiritual beings, but that animals are not – that we can walk a spiritual path, but they cannot? Many of the great spiritual Masters have seemed to love these beings called animals. Buddha said that: *When a man has pity on all living creatures, only then is he noble.*

Allah talks about bees being spiritual creatures and carrying divine messages to us. Jesus proclaimed: *Go into all the world and preach the Gospel to every creature.*

He didn't say just your fellow human beings. .... Of course, if we believed that animals were spiritual beings, just as we are, we would have to treat them with dignity. Maybe that's what some people are afraid of...

Ottoman Zar-Adusht Ha'nish (Islam)

It is strange to hear people talk of Humanitarianism, who are members of societies for the prevention of cruelty to children and animals, and who claim to be ALLAH-loving men and women, but whom nevertheless, encourage by their patronage the killing of animals merely to gratify the cravings of appetite.

Ovid (43 BC-17AD), Roman Poet

Oh, Ox, how great are thy desserts! A being without guile, harmless, simple, willing for work! Ungrateful and unworthy of the fruits of earth, Man his own farm laborer slays and smites with the axe that toil-worn neck that has so often renewed for him the face of the hard earth; so many harvests given!

Ovid (43 BC-17AD), Roman Poet

Alas, what wickedness to swallow flesh into our own flesh, to fatten our greedy bodies by cramming in other bodies, to have one living creature fed by the death of another!

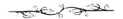

Ovid (43 BC-17AD), Roman Poet

Forbear, O mortals,
To spoil your bodies with such impious food! There is corn for
you, apples, whose weight bears down
The bending branches; there are grapes that swell
On the green vines, and pleasant herbs, and greens
Made mellow and soft with cooking; there is milt
And clover-honey. Earth is generous
With her provision, and her sustenance
Is very kind; she offers, for your tables,
Food that requires no bloodshed and no slaughter.

Thomas Paine (1737-1809), English born American Revolutionary Patriot and Writer: The Age of Reason

The moral duty of man consists of imitating the moral goodness and beneficence of God, manifested in the creation, toward all His creatures.

Thomas Paine (1737-1809), English born American Revolutionary Patriot and Writer

A long habit of not thinking a thing wrong, gives it a superficial appearance of being right, and raises at first a formidable outcry in defense of custom. But the tumult soon subsides.

Phil Pastoret

If you think dogs can't count, try putting three dog biscuits in your pocket and then giving Fido only two of them.

Rabbi Pinchas Peli

We cannot treat any living thing callously, and we are responsible for what happens to other beings, human or animal, even if we do not personally come into contact with them.

Joaquin Phoenix (1974 -): Actor and Activist

I was 3 years old - to this day it is a vivid memory. My family and I were on a boat, catching fish. As one fish was caught, he was writhing, and then he was thrown against the side of the boat. You couldn't disguise what it was. This was what we did to animals to eat them. The animal went from a living, vibrant creature fighting for life to a violent death. I recognized it, as did my brothers and sisters.

Rev. C.V. Pink, M.R.C.S., L.R.C.P., (Liberal Catholic Church): Extract from a transcript of a lecture: A Christian Ethic with reference to An Essay on Man by Alexander Pope (1688-1744), World Forum, Spring 1953

Our minds are in compartments and to preserve our comfort we see to it that the contents of different compartments do not get mixed. May I remind you that 'holiness' carries the meaning of 'wholeness,' so that he who aspires must needs see about breaking down these compartments. I hold that because of our kinship we have a clear ethical duty to protect animals from cruelty and sudden death, and not to eat them...anyone who accepts the idea of the One Life must accord to the animals the rights of younger brothers.

Plutarch (45-125AD), Famous Vegetarian Greek Philosopher, Historian and Biographer

I for my part do much marvel at what sort of feeling, soul or reason the first man with his mouth touched slaughter, and reached to his lips the flesh of a dead animal, and having set before people courses of ghastly corpses and ghosts, could give those parts the names of meat and victuals that but a little before lowed, cried, moved, and saw; how his sight could endure the blood of the slaughtered, flayed, and mangled bodies; how his smell could bear their scent; and how the very nastiness happened not to offend the taste while it chewed the sores of others, and participated of the sap and juices of deadly wounds

Plato (427?–347 B.C.) Famous Vegetarian Greek Philosopher (Student of Socrates)

The Gods created certain kinds of beings to replenish our bodies; they are the trees and the plants and the seeds.

Robert M. Pirsig, Zen and the Art of Motorcycle Maintenance

When a shepherd goes to kill a wolf, and takes his dog along to see the sport, he should take care to avoid mistakes. The dog has certain relationships to the wolf the shepherd may have forgotten.

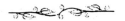

Plutarch (45-125AD), Famous Vegetarian Greek Philosopher, Historian and Biographer

But for the sake of some little mouthful of flesh, we deprive a soul of the sun, and light, and that proportion of life and time they had been born into the world to enjoy.

136

Plutarch (45-125AD), Famous Vegetarian Greek Philosopher, Historian and Biographer

But whence is it that a certain ravenousness and frenzy drives you in these happy days to pollute yourselves with blood, since you have such an abundance of things necessary for your subsistence? Why do you belie the earth as unable to maintain you? ...Are you not ashamed to mix tame fruits with blood and slaughter? You are indeed wont to call serpents, leopards, and lions, savage creatures; but yet yourselves are defiled with blood and come nothing behind them in cruelty. What they kill is their ordinary nourishment, but what you kill is your better fare.

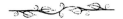

Plutarch (45-125AD), Famous Vegetarian Greek Philosopher, Historian and Biographer

For we eat not lions and wolves by way of revenge, but we let those go and catch the harmless and tame sort, such as have neither stings nor teeth to bite with, and slay them.

Plato (427?–347 B.C.) Famous Vegetarian Greek Philosopher (Student of Socrates)

We understand why children are afraid of darkness, but why are men [people] afraid of light?

Plutarch (45-125AD), Famous Vegetarian Greek Philosopher, Historian and Biographer

The obligations of law and equity reach only to mankind; but kindness and beneficence should be extended to the creatures of every species and these will flow from the breast of a true man, as streams that issue from the living fountain.

Plutarch (45-125AD), Famous Vegetarian Greek Philosopher, Historian and Biographer

But if you will contend that you were born to an inclination to such food as you have now a mind to eat, do you then yourself kill what you would eat. But do it yourself, without the help of a chopping knife, mallet, or axe - as wolves, bears, and lions do, who kill and eat at once. Rend an ox with thy teeth, worry a hog with thy mouth, tear a lamb or a hare in pieces and fall on and eat it alive as they do. But if though hadst rather stay until what thou eatest is to become dead and if thou art loath to force a soul out of its body, why then dost thou against Nature eat an animate thing?

Polish Proverb

The greatest love is a mother's; then a dog's; then a sweetheart's.

Plutarch (45-125AD), Famous Vegetarian Greek Philosopher, Historian and Biographer

Were it only to learn benevolence to humankind we should be merciful to other creatures.

Plutarch (45-125AD), Famous Vegetarian Greek Philosopher, Historian and Biographer: Extract from: On Eating Flesh

..I rather wonder both by what accident and in what state of mind the first man touched his mouth to gore and brought his lips to the flesh of a dead creature, set forth tables of dead, stale bodies, and ventured to call food and nourishment the parts that had before bellowed and cried, moved and lived.

Plutarch (45-125AD), Famous Vegetarian Greek Philosopher, Historian and Biographer: Extract from: On Eating Flesh

...To the Dolphin alone, beyond all other, nature has granted what the best philosophers seek: friendship for no advantage.

Plutarch (45-125AD), Famous Vegetarian Greek Philosopher, Historian and Biographer: Extract from: On Eating Flesh

How could eyes endure the slaughter when throats were slit and hides flayed and limbs torn from limb? How could his nose endure the stench? How was it that the pollution did not turn away his taste, which made contact with sores of others and sucked juices and serums from mortal wounds?

Plutarch (45-125AD), Famous Vegetarian Greek Philosopher, Historian and Biographer: Extract from: On Eating Flesh

It is certainly not lions or wolves that we eat out of self-defense; on the contrary, we ignore these and slaughter harmless, tame creatures without stings or teeth to harm us. For the sake of flesh we deprive them of sun, of light, of the duration of life to which they are entitled by birth and being.

Plutarch (45-125AD), Famous Vegetarian Greek Philosopher, Historian and Biographer: Extract from: On Eating Flesh

If you declare that you are naturally designed for such a diet, then first kill yourself what you want to eat. Do it, however, only through your own resources, unaided by cleaver or cudgel or any kind of axe.

Plutarch (45-125AD), Famous Vegetarian Greek Philosopher, Historian and Biographer

Though the boys throw stones at the frogs in sport, yet the frogs do not die in sport, but in earnest.

Poletti, Author

To be kind is to be courageous
To be great is to be compassionate.
To have love and reverence for all life including animals wild and domestic is to fully understand the purpose and divine nature of God.

Alex Poulos

I will not eat anything that walks, runs, skips, hops or crawls. God knows that I've crawled on occasion, and I'm glad that no one ate me.

Pope John Paul II

[St Francis] looks upon creation with the eyes of one who could recognize in it the marvelous work of the hand of God. His solicitous care, not only towards men, but also towards animals is a faithful echo of the love with which God in the beginning pronounced his 'fiat' which brought them into existence. We too are called to a similar attitude.

Porphyry, (232AD), Famous Vegetarian Greek Philosopher and Writer of Treatises: Extract from: On Abstinence from Animal Food

He who abstains from anything animate...will be much more careful not to injure those of his own species. For he who loves the genus will not hate any species of animals.

Rev. Humphrey Primatt (1736-1779), Anglican Priest: Extract from: A Dissertation on the Duty of Mercy and the Sin of Cruelty to Brute Animals.

Pain is pain, whether it is inflicted on man or on beast; and the creature that suffers it, whether man or beast, being sensible of the misery of it whilst it lasts, suffers Evil...

Porphyry, (232AD), Famous Vegetarian Greek Philosopher and Writer of Treatises

But to deliver animals to be slaughtered and cooked and thus be filled with murder, not for the sake of nutriment and satisfying the wants of nature, but making pleasure and gluttony the end of such conduct, is transcendently iniquitous and dire.

And is it not absurd, since we see that many of our own species live from sense alone, but do not possess intellect and reason; and since we also see that many of them surpass the most terrible of wild beasts in cruelty, anger, and rapine, being murderous of their children and their parents and also being tyrants and the tools of kings

[It is not ridiculous] to fancy that we ought to act justly towards these, but that no justice is due from us to the ox that ploughs, the dog that is fed with us, and the animals that nourish us with their milk and adorn our bodies with their wool?
Is not such an opinion most irrational and absurd?

Rev. Humphrey Primatt (1736-1779), Anglican Priest

...A cruel Christian is a monster of ingratitude, a scandal to his profession and beareth the name of Christ in vain...

Rev. Humphrey Primatt (1736-1779), Anglican Priest

We may pretend to what religion we please, but cruelty is atheism. We may make our boast of Christianity; but cruelty is infidelity. We may trust our orthodoxy, but cruelty is the worst of heresies.

Rev. Humphrey Primatt (1736-1779), Anglican Priest: From a Dissertation on the Duty of Mercy and the Sin of Cruelty to Brute Animals, 1776, (I-IV)

However men may differ as to speculative points of Religion, JUSTICE is a rule of universal extent and invariable obligation. We acknowledge this important truth in all matters in which MAN is concerned, but then we limit it to our own species only.

To rectify this mistaken notion is the design of this treatise, in which I have endeavored to prove, that as the Love and Mercy of God are over all of his works, from the highest rational to the lowest sensitive, our Love and Mercy are not to be confined within the circle of our own friends, acquaintances, and neighbours; nor limited to the more enlarged sphere of human nature, to creatures of our own rank, shape, and capacity.

But are to be extended to every object of the Love and Mercy of GOD the universal Parent; who, as he is righteous in all his ways, and holy in all his works, will undoubtedly require of Man, superior Man, a strict account of his conduct to every creature entrusted to his care, or coming in his way; and who will avenge every instance of wanton cruelty and oppression, in the day in which he will judge the world in RIGHTEOUSNESS.

142

Rev. Humphrey Primatt (1736-1779), Anglican Priest: A Dissertation on the Duty of Mercy and the Sin of Cruelty to Brute Animals, 1776, (53)

Whilst he lives [the brute] has a right to happiness.

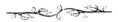

Rev. Humphrey Primatt (1736-1779), Anglican Priest

Let no views of profit, no compliance with custom, and no fear of the ridicule of the world, ever tempt thee to the least act of cruelty or injustice to any creature whatsoever. But let this be your invariable rule, everywhere, and at all times, to do unto others as, in their condition, you would be done unto.

Rev. Humphrey Primatt (1736-1779), Anglican Priest: A Dissertation on the Duty of Mercy and the Sin of Cruelty to Brute Animals, 1776, (47)

What should we think of a stout and strong Man that should exert his fury and barbarity on a helpless and innocent Babe? Should we not abhor and detest that man, as a mean, cowardly, and savage wretch, unworthy the stature and strength of a man? No less mean, cowardly, and savage is it, to abuse and torment the innocent Beast, who can neither help himself or avenge himself; and yet has as much right to happiness in this world as a child can have; nay, more right, if this world be his only inheritance.

Pythagoras (578-510 BC?) Famous Vegetarian Greek Philosopher and Mathematician and Founder of European Science and Philosophy

The animals share with us the privilege of having a soul.

Rev. Humphrey Primatt (1736-1779), Anglican Priest: A Dissertation on the Duty of Mercy and the Sin of Cruelty to Brute Animals, 1776, (177)

The laborious Beast of every kind, whether Ox, or Horse, or Ass, has a just right to every refreshment of nature.

Rev. Humphrey Primatt (1736-1779), Anglican Priest: A Dissertation on the Duty of Mercy and the Sin of Cruelty to Brute Animals, 1776, (147)

There are Three Instances of Regard, which the Creatures, who are instructed to our care, in consideration of their service, and dependence upon us, have an undoubted right to, and which on the principles of natural Religion they may justly demand of us; and these are FOOD, REST, and TENDER USAGE. These three demands of Food, Rest, and Tender Usage, the Goodness of the great GOD their Creator has been pleased to covenant for on their behalf, and to enjoin and ratify in his written Laws.

Rev. Humphrey Primatt (1736-1779), Anglican Priest: A Dissertation on the Duty of Mercy and the Sin of Cruelty to Brute Animals, 1776, (151-2)

The soil is the property of GOD, the Lord Paramount of the Manor, who hath made the grass to grow for the CATTLE. The grass of the field therefore is no gift of yours to them; it is their right; their property; it was provided for them, and given to them, before man was created.

Proverbs12:10

A righteous man has regard for the life of his beast.

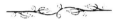

Pythagoras (578-510 BC?) Famous Vegetarian Greek Philosopher and Mathematician and Founder of European Science and Philosophy

As long as man continues to be the ruthless destroyer of lower livings beings,

He will never know health or peace.

For as long as men massacre animals, they will kill each other.

Indeed, he who sows the seed of murder and pain cannot reap joy and love.

Rev. Humphrey Primatt (1736-1779), Anglican Priest: A Dissertation on the Duty of Mercy and the Sin of Cruelty to Brute Animals, 1776, (253)

To neglect, or abuse, or ill treat our own Cattle, is cruelty of a heinous nature; because they have a right to our Care and Tenderness: and if any man Provides not for his own, and especially for those of his own house, he hath denied the Faith, and is worse than an Infidel. But our Mercy and Regard is not to rest there. It is further our duty to be always ready to relieve and succour the Miserable, whether known or unknown to us. Any Beast in distress, be it Ox, or Ass, or Sheep, or other Animal, has a claim upon us of Assistance.

Rev. Humphrey Primatt (1736-1779), Anglican Priest: A Dissertation on the Duty of Mercy and the Sin of Cruelty to Brute Animals, 1776, (197-8)

> For as SABBATH was ordained for beast as well as man, though the beast is not capable of keeping the Sabbath as a day of Sanctification, he hath by the command of God a right to a Sabbath as a day of Rest and Blessing.

Rev. Humphrey Primatt (1736-1779), Anglican Priest: A Dissertation on the Duty of Mercy and the Sin of Cruelty to Brute Animals, 1776, (259-60; 270-1)

> No Creature is so insignificant, but whilst it had Life, it has a Right to Happiness. To deprive it of Happiness is Injustice; and to put it to unnecessary Pain is Cruelty.
>
> It is very unreasonable therefore, if not foolish in men, to estimate the degree of the sin of cruelty to any creature by the value we set upon the creature itself; or to suppose that difference of size, or difference of beauty, are foundations of real difference as to the feelings of Brutes.
>
> A Fly had feeling as well as an Ox; and a Toad has a much right of happiness as a Canary Bird; for the same GOD made the Ox, and the Fly and the Toad and the Bird... For Cruelty to a Brute is odious and abominable, whether it be to a Beast, a Bird, or a Fish, or a Worm. Be the creature never so insignificant in our estimation, we cannot put it to any degree of pain without a violation of the Laws of Nature; because every living creature is the work of the GOD of Nature.

Pythagoras (578-510 BC?) Famous Vegetarian Greek Philosopher and Mathematician and Founder of European Science and Philosophy

If men with fleshly mortals must be fed,
And chaw with bleeding teeth the breathing bread;
What else is this but to devour our guests?
And barbarously renew Cyclopean feasts?
While Earth not only can your needs supply,
But, lavish of her store, provides for luxury;
A guiltless feast administer with ease,
And without blood is prodigal to please.

Pythagoras (578-510 BC?) Famous Vegetarian Greek Philosopher and Mathematician and Founder of European Science and Philosophy

Do not defile your bodies with sinful foods. The earth affords you a lavish supply of riches, of innocent foods, and offers you banquets that involve no bloodshed or slaughter.

Pythagoras (578-510 BC?) Famous Vegetarian Greek Philosopher and Mathematician and Founder of European Science and Philosophy

Alas, what wickedness to swallow flesh into our own flesh, to fatten our greedy bodies by cramming in other bodies, to have one living creature fed by the death of another!

Gilda Radner

I think dogs are the most amazing creatures; they give unconditional love. For me they are the role model for being alive.

Rabindranath, (1861-1941), Hindu Poet Winner of the Nobel Prize, Composer of India's National Anthem

We manage to swallow flesh only because we do not think of the cruel and sinful thing we do. There are many crimes which are the creation of man himself, the wrongfulness of which is put down to his divergence from habit, custom, or tradition. But cruelty is not of these. It is a fundamental sin, and admits of no arguments or nice distinctions.

If only we do not allow our heart to grow callous it protects against cruelty, is always clearly heard; and yet we go on perpetrating cruelties easily, merrily, all of us - in fact, anyone who does not join in is dubbed a crank...If, after our pity is aroused, we persist in throttling our feelings simply in order to join others in preying upon life, we insult all that is good in us. I have decided to try a vegetarian diet.

Tom Regan, Author and Educator

All of us engaged in the struggle for animal rights have a tendency to forget who we once were. Most of us once ate meat, for example, or unblinkingly dissected nonhuman animals in the lab during high school or college biology courses. Probably we went to a zoo or an aquarium and had a good time. Some of us hunted or fished and enjoyed that, too. The plain fact is it is not just society that needs changing. The struggle for animal rights is also a struggle with self.

What we are trying to do is transform the moral zombie society would like us to be into the morally advanced being we are capable of becoming. All liberation movements have this common theme. That's only one of the ways our Movement resembles other rights movements of the past.

Tom Regan, Author and Educator: Empty Cages, (P96)

Turning pigs into commodities, the deliberate reduction of them into mere things, characterizes the mind-set of the industry. 'The breeding sow should be thought of, and treated as, a valuable piece of machinery,' advises a corporate manager of Wall's Meat Company, 'whose function is to pump out baby pigs like a sausage machine.' Say what you will, the hog industry is mighty good at this.

Rabbi Nachmanides, (1184-1270)

Living creatures possess a moving soul and a certain spiritual superiority which, in this respect make them similar to those who possess intellect (people) and they have the power of affecting their welfare and their food and they flee from pain and death.

Tom Regan, Author and Educator: Empty Cages, (P19)

With rare exceptions, Animal Rights Advocates are for love of
family and country, for human rights and justice, for human
freedom and equality, for compassion and mercy, for peace and
tolerance, for special concern for those with special needs
(children, the enfeebled, the elderly, among others), for a clean,
sustainable environment, for the rights of our children's
children's children - our future generations. In a word, the vast
majority are Norman Rockwell Americans, straight off his famous
Thanksgiving cover for the old Saturday Evening Post, only with
this noteworthy difference. 'We'll pass on the turkey, thank you.
We don't eat our friends.'

Tom Regan, Author and Educator: Empty Cages, (P149)

When all the rhetorical dust settles, the real rush for the sport
hunter comes from the kill. Any doubt about this, just look
through any of the hunting magazines at the local newsstand. The
hunters pictured in those pages, displaying their dead wares,
smiling from ear to ear, could not be happier. If we asked them to
pose with beanbag chairs, it just wouldn't be the same.

Tom Regan, Author and Educator: Empty Cages, (P118)

Beginning in 1987, Americans were outraged when the Humane
Society of the United States exposed the international trade in cat
and dog fur, especially when they learned that garments in
American stores were trimmed or lined with fur from these
animals . . . Cats and dogs should not have their fur stolen from
them, Americans protested. It's their fur; it belongs to them, not
to us.

Animal Rights Advocates could not agree more. To kill cats and
dogs for their fur is both uncivilized and unethical. It's just that
we think the same is true when the fur is stolen from any animal.

Tom Regan, Author and Educator: Empty Cages, (P152)

In rodeos, calves can reach speeds up to thirty miles an hour before they are lassoed ('clotheslined'); often they are jerked over backward and slammed to the ground ... The faster they are running at the time, the harder they are pulled backward. And the harder they are pulled backward, the more their necks are wrenched and the greater the force with which they hit the ground. Some calves do not do encores. It's one performance and out ...

So here we have today's brave cowboy, bending over and tying up a frightened, dazed, disoriented baby (the animals are all of four or five months old), with neck and back injuries, bruises, broken bones, and internal hemorrhages. Are those who are working to abolish rodeo in general, calf roping in particular, just overwrought, emotionally unbalanced calf huggers?

Tom Regan, Author and Educator: Empty Cages, (P110)

According to Fur Commission USA, mink raised on fur 'ranches' are treated 'humanely,' meaning with compassion, kindness, and mercy. In fact, they are 'the best cared-for livestock' in the world, a statement that, tragically, just might be true.

Compared with veal calves, hogs, and chickens raised in confinement, those lucky mink who spend their waking hours pacing back and forth, jumping up the sides of cages, and rotating their heads, are leading a country club existence. May God forgive us.

Tom Regan, Author and Educator: Empty Cages, (P115)

Despite official assurances to the contrary, many seals are skinned while still alive. It would be a relief to learn that this happens rarely, though of course it should not happen at all. The bad news is it happens a lot. An independent scientific study, conducted in 2001 by a team of veterinarians, concluded that 42 per cent of the seals were skinned alive. That works out to approximately 130,000.

Tom Regan, Author and Educator: Empty Cages, (P189)

On a daily basis, animals are drowned, suffocated and starved to death; they have their limbs severed and their organs crushed; they are burned, exposed to radiation, and used in experimental surgeries.

They are shocked, raised in isolation, exposed to weapons of mass destruction, and rendered blind or paralyzed; they are the given heart attacks, ulcers, paralysis, and seizures; they are forced to inhale tobacco smoke, drink alcohol, and ingest various drugs, such as heroine and cocaine. And they say Animal Rights Advocates are violent?

The violence done by Animal Rights Advocates (almost all of it taking the form of property destruction) is nothing compared to the violence done by the world's vivisectors, a raindrop compared to an ocean. Just because a profession is legal, perhaps even (as in the case of vivisection) prestigious does not mean it is nonviolent. On a day-to-day basis, the greatest amount of violence in the world occurs because of what humans do to other animals. That the violence is legally protected only serves to make matters worse.

Tom Regan, Author and Educator: Empty Cages, (P137)

Free dolphins swim up to forty miles a day and can dive to depths of more than a quarter mile. In their natural environment, they live in extended social groups (pods) and find their way around in an ever-changing, challenging environment via echolocation. (They 'see' by hearing). Once in captivity, these animals are confined in concrete tanks (sometimes measuring as little as twenty-four feet long by twenty-four feet wide by six feet deep) or in small sea-cages.

There are no pods here. Nothing changes in any significant way in this desolate world. No natural challenges are faced. Nothing naturally interesting is found because there is nothing naturally interesting to be found. To speak candidly, it is worse than disingenuous; it is shameful that anyone would stand before us and say, 'We really and truly care about the welfare of our dolphins,' animals who have nothing to locate, no family to be with, no place to dive, no miles to swim.

Tom Regan, Author and Educator: Empty Cages, (P100-101)

Symbolic of the 'humane' treatment animals receive at slaughterhouses is the plight of so-called downers. These are animals who are so sick or so badly injured that they cannot stand up or walk. Depending on conditions at the plant, downers can lay on the ground for a day or more, without water, food, or veterinary care. Whether dead or alive, eventually they are pulled inside the slaughterhouse by chains or hoisted by a forklift.

A Zogby poll found that 79 per cent of the adults interviewed opposed the slaughter of downers. Not the dairy industry, which lobbied vigorously to delete legislation before the Congress in 2001 that aspired to ban the sale of downers. Why would the dairy industry oppose such minimal legislation? Because most downed animals are dairy cows who can be slaughtered for their meat after they no longer can produce milk.

Tom Regan, Author and Educator: Empty Cages, (P127)

An opportunity to expand animal consciousness presents itself if we look behind the eyes of wild animals trained to perform in circuses. In the wild, the home range for African lions and Indian male tigers varies from 8 to 156 square miles; for Siberian male tigers, up to 400 square miles.

For the sake of comparison, consider that San Francisco and Boston occupy 47 and 48 square miles, respectively; Chicago, 227; New York City, including all five boroughs, 309 square miles. No sensible person can believe that circuses provide lions and tigers with a caged environment of 'sufficient space,' one that offers the animals 'adequate freedom of movement.'

Tom Regan, Author and Educator: Empty Cages, (P156)

Day-to-day life for racing greyhounds is characterized by chronic deprivation. Dogs are confined in small crates, some measuring three feet by three feet. On days when they are not racing, the animals can be crated for up to twenty-two hours, sometimes stacked in tiers. Except when eating, they are muzzled . . .

As for why they are muzzled, the explanation is an expression of the industry's commitment to humane treatment. After all, if their muzzles were removed, the dogs could injure their mouth, teeth, or gums when they gnaw on their wire cage. In other words, the industry's remedy for one kind of deprivation (keeping the dogs caged) is to impose another kind of deprivation (keeping them muzzled), the better to treat them more humanely.

Agnes Repplier

Our dogs will love and admire the meanest of us, and feed our colossal vanity with their uncritical homage.

John Robbins, Author and Lecturer

It is increasingly obvious that environmentally sustainable solutions to world hunger can only emerge as people eat more plant foods and fewer animal products. To me it is deeply moving that the same food choices that give us the best chance to eliminate world hunger are also those that take the least toll on the environment, contribute the most to our long-term health, are the safest, and are also, far and away, the most compassionate towards our fellow creatures.

William C. Roberts, M.D., Editor of The American Journal of Cardiology

When we kill the animals to eat them, they end up killing us because their flesh, which contains cholesterol and saturated fat, was never intended for human beings.

John Robbins, Author and Lecturer

Awareness is bad for the meat business. Conscience is bad for the meat business. Sensitivity to life is bad for the meat business. DENIAL, however, the meat business finds indispensable.

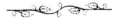

Will Rogers

If you get to thinking you're a person of some influence, try ordering somebody else's dog around.

Mabel Louise Robinson

From the dog's point of view, his master is an elongated and abnormally cunning dog.

Richard of Wyche (1197-1253), Bishop of Chichester: On seeing animals being killed for food

> You, who are innocent, what have you done worthy of [murderous] death!

Robert K. Ressler, a former FBI Agent and Author who coined the term: 'Serial Killer.' This is what he said about the violent offenders that he profiled:

> These are the kids who never learned it's wrong to poke out a puppy's eyes.

Romain Rolland (1866-1944), French Novelist, Dramatist, Essayist, Mystic and Pacifist: He received the Nobel Prize for Literature, 1915

> To a man whose mind is free, there is something even more intolerable in the sufferings of animals than in the sufferings of man. For with the latter it is at least admitted that suffering is evil and that the man who causes it is a criminal. But thousands of animals are uselessly butchered every day without a shadow of remorse. If any man were to refer to it, he would be thought ridiculous. And that is the unpardonable crime.

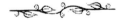

Romain Rolland (1866-1944), French Novelist, Dramatist, Essayist, Mystic and Pacifist: He received the Nobel Prize for Literature, 1915

> Thousands of animals are butchered every day without a shadow of remorse. It cries vengeance upon all the human race.

Andy Rooney

If dogs could talk, it would take a lot of the fun out of owning one.

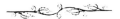

Andy Rooney

The average dog is a nicer person than the average person.

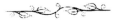

Eleanor Roosevelt, Former First Lady of the United States of America

It seems to me of great importance to teach children respect for life. Towards this end, experiments on living animals in classrooms should be stopped. To encourage cruelty in the name of science can only destroy the finer emotions of affection and sympathy, and breed an unfeeling callousness in the young towards suffering in all living creatures.

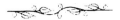

Steven Rosen: Extract from Diet for Transcendence, (Introduction)

...Universal religious thought promotes universal compassion and condemns the opposite - the unnecessary slaughter of animals - as fundamentally irreligious.

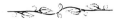

Jean-Jacques Rousseau (1712-1778), Swiss, French Philosopher and Author

Everything is good as it leaves the hands of the Author of things; everything degenerates in the hands of man.

Jean-Jacques Rousseau (1712-1778), Swiss, French Philosopher and Author

Nature never deceives us; it is always we, who deceive ourselves.

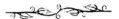

Jean-Jacques Rousseau (1712-1778), Swiss, French Philosopher and Author

Man is born free; and everywhere he is in chains.

Jean-Jacques Rousseau (1712-1778), Swiss, French Philosopher and Author

A country cannot subsist well without liberty, nor liberty without virtue. [Compassion to all animals, human and non-human represents virtue.]

Jean-Jacques Rousseau (1712-1778), Swiss, French Philosopher and Author

The animals you eat are not those who devour others; you do not eat the carnivorous beasts, you take them as your pattern. You only hunger after sweet and gentle creatures who harm no one, follow you, serve you, and are devoured by you as the reward of their service.

Jean-Jacques Rousseau (1712-1778), Swiss-born French Philosopher and Author

What wisdom can you find that is greater than kindness?

Jean-Jacques Rousseau (1712-1778), Swiss, French Philosopher and Author

One could wish no easier death than that of Socrates, calmly discussing philosophy with his friends; one could fear nothing worse than that of Jesus, dying in torment, among the insults, the mockery, the curses of the whole nation. In the midst of these terrible sufferings, Jesus prays for his cruel murderers. Yes, if the life and death of Socrates are those of a philosopher, the life and death of Christ are those of a God.

Geoffrey Rudd, English Author, Anthropologist and Secretary of the International Vegetarian Union, 1965

No sensitive person would eat flesh if he or she had to do the skull-breaking, slaughtering, strangling, blood-letting, skinning and disemboweling, and live in the stench and among the agonized cries of the victims.

Dr Robert Runcie, Archbishop of Canterbury

In the end, a lack of regard for the life and well-being of an animal must bring with it a lowering of man's self-respect and it is integral to our Christian faith that this world is God's world and that man is a trustee and steward of God's creation who must render up an account for his stewardship.

John Ruskin (1819-1900)

Without the perfect sympathy with the animals around them, no gentleman's education, no Christian education, could be of any possible use.

Dr Carl Sagan and Ann Dryan: Extract from Shadows of Forgotten Ancestors, 1992

> Humans – who enslave, castrate, experiment on, and fillet other animals - have had an understandable penchant for pretending animals do not feel pain. A sharp distinction between humans and "animals" is essential if we are to bend them to our will, make them work for us, wear them, eat them – without any disquieting tinges of guilt or regret. It is unseemly of us, who often behave so unfeelingly toward other animals, to contend that only humans can suffer. The behavior of other animals renders such pretensions specious. They are just too much like us.

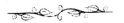

Translation of Sahih Bukhari, Ablutions (Wudu) Vol. 1, Book 4, No 174. (Islam)

> The Prophet said: 'A man saw a dog eating mud due to (the severity of thirst). So, that man took a shoe (and filled it) with water and kept on pouring the water for the dog till it quenched its thirst. So Allah approved of his deed and made him to enter Paradise.'

Henry S. Salt, (1851-1939), British Philanthropist and Reformer: Friend of Gandhi and George Bernard Shaw

> The cattle [transport] of present day reproduce, in an aggravated form, some of the worst horrors of the slave-ships of fifty years back...The present system of killing animals for food is a very cruel and barbarous one, and a direct outrage on what I have termed the 'humanities of diet.'

Henry S. Salt, (1851-1939), British Philanthropist and Reformer, colleague of Gandhi and George Bernard Shaw

> Vegetarianism is the diet of the future, as flesh-food is the diet of the past. In that striking and common contrast, a fruit shop side by side with a butcher's, we have a most significant object lesson.
>
> There, on the one hand, are the barbarities of a savage custom - the headless carcasses, stiffened into a ghastly semblance of life, the joints and steaks and gobbets with their sickening odor the harsh grating of the bone-saw, and the dull thud of the chopper - a perpetual crying protest against the horrors of flesh-eating.
>
> And as if this were not witness sufficient, here close alongside is a wealth of golden fruit, a sight to make a poet happy, the only food that is entirely congenial to the physical structure and the natural instincts of mankind that can entirely satisfy the highest human aspirations.
>
> Can we doubt, as we gaze at this contrast, that whatever immediate steps may need to be gradually taken, whatever difficulties to be overcome, the path of progression from the barbarities to the humanities of diet lies clear and unmistakable before us?

Dr Carl Sagan, Faculty Adviser for the Cornell Students, USA, for the Ethical Treatment of Animals ~ COSMOS, Episode 'Blues for a Red Planet'

> If there is life, then I believe we should do nothing to disturb that life. Mars then, belongs to the Martians, even if they are microbes.

Henry S. Salt, (1851-1939), British Philanthropist and Reformer: Friend of Gandhi and George Bernard Shaw: From: The Humanities of Diet

> This logic of the larder is the very negation of a true reverence for life, for it implies that the real lover of animals is he whose larder is fullest of them:
>
> He, prayest best, who eatest best.
> All things both great and small.
> It is the philosophy of the wolf, the shark, the cannibal.

Henry S. Salt, (1851-1939), British Philanthropist and Reformer: Friend of Gandhi and George Bernard Shaw

> ...I suggest that in proportion as man is truly "humanized," not by schools of cookery but by schools of thought, he will abandon the barbarous habit of his flesh-eating ancestors, and will make gradual progress towards a purer, simpler, more humane, and therefore more civilized diet - system.

Henry S. Salt, (1851-1939), British Philanthropist and Reformer: Friend of Gandhi and George Bernard Shaw

> It is not THIS bloodshed or THAT bloodshed that must cease, but ALL bloodshed - all wonton infliction of pain or death.

Henry S. Salt, (1851-1939), British Philanthropist and Reformer: Friend of Gandhi and George Bernard Shaw

> The cause of each and all of the evils that afflict the world is the same - the general lack of humanity, the lack of the knowledge that all sentient life is akin, and that he who injures a fellow being is in fact doing injury to himself.

Henry S. Salt, (1851-1939), British Philanthropist and Reformer: Friend of Gandhi and George Bernard Shaw

> In spite of their boasted progress in sciences and arts, my countrymen are still practically ignorant of the real kinship which exists between mankind and the other races, and of the duties which this kinship implies.
> They are still the victims of that old anthropocentric superstition which pictures man as the centre of the universe, and separated from the inferior animals - mere playthings made for his august pleasure and amusement - by a deep intervening gulf.

Arthur Schopenhauer (1788-1860), German Philosopher

> The assumption that animals are without rights and the illusion that our treatment of them has no moral significance is a positively outrageous example of Western crudity and barbarity. Universal compassion is the only guarantee of morality.

Arthur Schopenhauer (1788-1860), German Philosopher

> Compassion is the basis of all morality.

Arthur Schopenhauer (1788-1860), German Philosopher, quoted from 'On the Basis of Morality'

I know of no more beautiful prayer than that which the Hindus of old used in closing: May all that have life be delivered from suffering.

Arthur Schopenhauer (1788-1860), German Philosopher

Since compassion for animals is so intimately associated with goodness of character, it may be confidently asserted that whoever is cruel to animals cannot be a good man.

Stanley Sapon

Veganism acknowledges the intrinsic legitimacy of all life. It recognizes no hierarchy of acceptable suffering among sentient creatures. It is no more acceptable to kill creatures with primitive nervous systems than those with highly developed nervous systems. The value of life to its possessor is the same, whether it be the life of the clam, a crayfish, a carp, a cow, a chicken, or child.

Knut Scharnhorst, Physician and Author: Christopher's Garden

If the pioneering woman had possessed enough insight to recognise the basic problem and its solution:- the family's return to the peaceful, worry-free, disease-free existence of the garden-life, with its fruit, nuts, greens and grain-raising, not only would women have been freed, but the whole human race with her!

Arthur Schopenhauer (1788-1860), German Philosopher: On the Basis of Morality

Because Christian morality leaves animals out of account, they are at once outlawed in philosophical morals; they are mere 'things,' mere means to any ends whatsoever. They can therefore be used for vivisection, hunting, coursing, bullfights, and horse racing, and can be whipped to death as they struggle along with heavy carts of stone. Shame on such a morality that is worthy of pariahs, and that fails to recognize the eternal essence that exists in every living thing, and shines forth with inscrutable significance from all eyes that see the sun!

Arthur Schopenhauer (1788-1860), German Philosopher

All truth goes through three stages. First it is ridiculed. Then it is violently opposed. Finally, it is accepted as self-evident.

Arthur Schopenhauer (1788-1860), German Philosopher: On the Will in Nature, Physiology and Pathology

Unlike the intellect, it [the Will] does not depend on the perfection of the organism, but is essentially the same in all animals as that which is known to us so intimately. Accordingly, the animal has all the emotions of humans, such as joy, grief, fear, anger, love, hatred, strong desire, envy, and so on. The great difference between human and animal rests solely on the intellect's degrees of perfection.

Rev. Dr. Albert Schweitzer (1875-1965), German Physician, Medical Missionary, Theologian, Musician, Author and Nobel Prize Winner, 1952

It is good to maintain and cherish life; it is evil to destroy...life.

Rev. Dr. Albert Schweitzer (1875-1965), German Physician and Medical Missionary, Theologian, Musician, Author and Nobel Prize Winner, 1952

Until he extends the circle of his compassion to all living things, Man will not himself find peace.

Professor Richard H Schwartz

Animals are part of God's creation and people have special responsibilities to them. The Jewish tradition clearly indicates that we are forbidden to be cruel to animals and that we are to treat them with compassion.

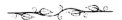

Rev. Dr. Albert Schweitzer (1875-1965), German Physician, Medical Missionary, Theologian, Musician, Author and Nobel Prize Winner, 1952

The very fact that the animal, as a victim of research, has in his pain rendered such services to suffering, men, has itself created a new and unique relation of solidarity between him and ourselves. The result is that a fresh obligation is laid on each of us to do as much good as we possibly can to all creatures in all sorts of circumstances. When I help an insect out of his troubles all that I do is to attempt to remove some of the guilt contracted through these crimes against animals.

Rev. Dr. Albert Schweitzer (1875-1965), German Physician, Medical Missionary, Theologian, Musician, Author and Nobel Prize Winner, 1952

A man is really ethical only when he obeys the constraint laid on him to help all life which he is able to succor and when he goes out of his way to avoid injuring anything living. He does not ask how far this or that life deserves sympathy as valuable in itself, or how far it is capable of feeling. To him life as such is sacred. He shatters no ice crystal that sparkles in the sun, tears no leaf from its tree, breaks off no flower and is careful not to crush any insect as he walks. If he works by lamplight on a summer evening, he prefers to keep the window shut and to breathe stifling air rather than to see insect after insect fall on his table with singed and sinking wings.

Rev. Dr. Albert Schweitzer (1875-1965), German Physician, Medical Missionary, Theologian, Musician, Author and Nobel Prize Winner, 1952

There slowly grew up in me an unshakable conviction that we have no right to inflict suffering and death on another living creature, unless there is some unavoidable necessity for it.

Rev. Dr. Albert Schweitzer (1875-1965), German Physician, Medical Missionary, Theologian, Musician, Author and Nobel Prize Winner, 1952

We are compelled by the commandment of love contained in our hearts and thought and proclaimed by Jesus, to give rein to our natural sympathy for animals. We are also compelled to help them and spare them suffering.

Rev. Dr. Albert Schweitzer (1875-1965), German Physician, Medical Missionary, Theologian, Musician, Author and Nobel Prize Winner, 1952

I must interpret the life about me as I interpret the life that is my own. My life is full of meaning to me.
The life around me must be full of significance to itself. If I am to expect others to respect my life, then I must respect the other life I see, however strange it may be to mine. ...We need a boundless ethics which will include the animals also.

Rev. Dr. Albert Schweitzer (1875-1965), German Physician, Medical Missionary, Theologian, Musician, Author and Nobel Prize Winner, 1952

Whenever any animal is forced into the service of man, the sufferings which it has to bear on that account is the concern of every one of us. No-one ought to permit, in so far as he can prevent it, pain or suffering for which he will not take the responsibility. No one ought to rest at ease in the thought that in so doing he would mix himself up in affairs which are not his business.

Let no-one shirk the burden of his responsibility. When there is so much maltreatment of animals, when the cries of thirsting creatures go up unnoticed from the railway truck, when there is so much roughness in our slaughterhouses, when in our kitchen so many animals suffer horrible deaths from unskillful hands, when animals endure unheard-of agonies from heartless men, or are delivered to the dreadful play of children, then we are all guilty and must bear the blame.

Rev. Dr. Albert Schweitzer (1875-1965), German Physician, Medical Missionary, Theologian, Musician, Author and Nobel Prize Winner, 1952

> The thinking man must oppose all cruel customs no matter how deeply rooted in tradition and surrounded by a halo. When we have a choice, we must avoid bringing torment and injury in to the life of another, even the lowliest creature; to do so is to renounce our manhood and shoulder a guilt which nothing justifies.

Rev. Dr. Albert Schweitzer (1875-1965), German Physician, Medical Missionary, Theologian, Musician, Author and Nobel Prize Winner, 1952

> We need a boundless ethic which will include the animals also. The ethics of respect for life makes us keep on the lookout together for opportunities of bringing some sort of help to animals, to make up for the great miseries men inflict on them.

Rev. Dr. Albert Schweitzer (1875-1965), German Physician, Medical Missionary, Theologian, Musician, Author and Nobel Prize Winner, 1952: Nobel Peace Prize Address: The Problem of Peace in the World Today

> The human spirit is not dead. It lives on in secret.....It has come to believe that compassion, in which all ethics must take root, can only attain its full breadth and depth if it embraces all living creatures and does not limit itself to mankind.

Rev. Dr. Albert Schweitzer (1875-1965), German Physician, Medical Missionary, Theologian, Musician, Author and Nobel Prize Winner, 1952

Anyone who has accustomed himself to regard the life of any living creature as worthless is in danger of arriving also at the idea of worthless human lives.

Rev. Dr. Albert Schweitzer (1875-1965), German Physician, Medical Missionary, Theologian, Musician, Author and Nobel Prize Winner, 1952

We must never permit the voice of humanity within us to be silenced. It is man's sympathy with all creatures that first makes him truly a man.

Rev. Dr. Albert Schweitzer (1875-1965), German Physician, Medical Missionary, Theologian, Musician, Author and Nobel Prize Winner, 1952

The man who has become a thinking being feels a compulsion to give every will-to-` live the reverence for life that he gives his own.

Rev. Dr. Albert Schweitzer (1875-1965), German Physician, Medical Missionary, Theologian, Musician, Author and Nobel Prize Winner, 1952

Any religion or philosophy which is not based on a respect for life is not a true religion or philosophy.

Rev. Dr. Albert Schweitzer (1875-1965), German Physician, Medical Missionary, Theologian, Musician, Author and Nobel Prize Winner, 1952

The quiet conscience is an invention of the devil.

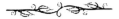

Rev. Dr. Albert Schweitzer (1875-1965), German Physician, Medical Missionary, Theologian, Musician, Author and Nobel Prize Winner, 1952

The time will come when public opinion will no longer tolerate amusements based on the mistreatment and killing of animals. The time will come, but when? When will we reach the point that hunting, the pleasure in killing animals for sport, will be regarded as a mental aberration?

Rev. Dr. Albert Schweitzer (1875-1965), German Physician, Medical Missionary, Theologian, Musician, Author and Nobel Prize Winner, 1952

Very little of the great cruelty shown by men can really be attributed to cruel instinct. Most of it comes from thoughtlessness or inherited habit. The roots of cruelty, therefore, are not so much strong as widespread. But the time must come wherein humanity protected by custom and thoughtlessness will succumb before humanity championed by thought.

Let us work that this time may come. The quiet conscience is an invention of the devil. Until he extends the circle of his compassion to all living things, man will not himself find peace. It is man's sympathy with all creatures that first makes him truly a man.

Rev. Dr. Albert Schweitzer (1875-1965), German Physician, Medical Missionary, Theologian, Musician, Author and Nobel Prize Winner, 1952: From: Out of My Life and Thought

Affirmation of life is the spiritual act by which man ceases to live unreflectively and begins to devote himself to his life with reverence in order to raise it to its true value. To affirm life is to deepen, to make more inward, and to exalt the will to live. At the same time the man who has become a thinking being feels a compulsion to give to every will-to-live the same reverence for life that he gives to his own.

He experiences that other life in his own. He accepts as being good: to preserve life, to promote life, to raise to its highest value life which is capable of development; and as being evil: to destroy life, to injure life, to repress life which is capable of development. This is the absolute, fundamental principle of the moral, and it is a necessity of thought.

Rev. Dr. Albert Schweitzer (1875-1965), German Physician, Medical Missionary, Theologian, Musician, Author and Nobel Prize Winner, 1952

It is the fate of every truth to be an object of ridicule when it is first acclaimed. It was once considered foolish to suppose that black men were really human beings and ought to be treated as such...

Today it is considered as exaggeration to proclaim constant respect for every form of life as being the serious demand of a rational ethic. But the time is coming when people will be amazed that the human race existed so long before it recognized that thoughtless injury to life is incompatible with real ethics. Ethics is in its unqualified form extended responsibility to everything that has life.

Rev. Dr. Albert Schweitzer (1875-1965), German Physician, Medical Missionary, Theologian, Musician, Author and Nobel Prize Winner, 1952

It is not always granted to the sower to live to see the harvest. All work that is worth anything is done in - FAITH.

Rev. Dr. Albert Schweitzer (1875-1965), German Physician, Medical Missionary, Theologian, Musician, Author and Nobel Prize Winner, 1952

Think occasionally of the suffering of which you spare yourself the sight.

Sefer Ha Chinuch, Mitzvah 596

When a man becomes accustomed to have pity upon animals...his soul will likewise grow accustomed to be kind to human beings.

Seneca (4 BC-65 AD), Famous Vegetarian Roman Philosopher, Statesman and Dramatist

If true, the Pythagorean principles as to abstaining from flesh foster innocence; if ill-founded they at least teach us frugality, and what loss have you in losing your cruelty? I merely deprive you of the food of lions and vultures.

We shall recover our sound reason only if we shall separate ourselves from the herd- the very fact of the approbation of the multitude is a proof of the unsoundness of the opinion or practice. Let us ask what is best, not what is customary. Let us love temperance - let us be just - let us refrain from bloodshed.

Seneca (4 BC-65 AD), Famous Vegetarian Roman Philosopher, Statesman and Dramatist

It is not because things are difficult that we do not dare; it is because we do not dare that they are difficult.

Richard Serjeant, Author of the Spectrum of Pain, Published in 1969

Every particle of factual evidence supports the factual contention that the higher mammalian vertebrates experience pain sensations at least as acute as our own. To say that they feel pain less because they are lower animals is an absurdity; it can easily be shown that many of their senses are far more acute than ours - visual acuity in certain birds, hearing in most wild animals, and touch in others; these animals depend more than we do today on the sharpest possible awareness of a hostile environment.

Apart from the complexity of the cerebral cortex (which does not directly perceive pain) their nervous systems are almost identical to ours and their reaction to pain remarkably similar, though lacking (so far as we know) the philosophical and moral overtones. The emotional element is all too evident, mainly in the form of fear and anger.

Anna Sewell, Author of Black Beauty

There is no religion without love, and people may talk as much as they like about their religion, but if it does not teach them to be good and kind to beasts as well as man it is all a sham.

William Shakespeare (1564–1616), English Poet and Playwright

To thine own self be true.

William Shakespeare (1564–1616), English Poet and Playwright: From The Merchant of Venice

The quality of mercy is not strained;

It droppeth as gently as the rain from heaven upon the place beneath;

It is twice blessed:

It blesseth him that gives and him that takes.

William Shakespeare (1564–1616), English Poet and Playwright

Peace above all earthly dignities: a still and quiet conscience.

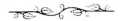

George Bernard Shaw (1856-1950), Irish Playwright and Critic: Received the Nobel Prize for Literature (1925) and an Oscar (1938) for his work on the film Pygmalion

My situation is a solemn one: life is offered to me on the condition of eating beefsteaks. But death is better than cannibalism. My will contains directions for my funeral, which will be followed, not by mourning coaches, but by oxen, sheep, flocks of poultry, and a small traveling aquarium of live fish, all wearing white scarves in honor of the man who perished rather than eat his fellow creatures. It will be, without the exception of Noah's Ark, the most remarkable thing of its kind ever seen.

George Bernard Shaw (1856-1950), Irish Playwright and Critic: Received the Nobel Prize for Literature (1925) and an Oscar (1938) for his work on the film Pygmalion

God has given us a world that nothing but our own folly keeps from being a paradise.

George Bernard Shaw (1856-1950), Irish Playwright and Critic: Received the Nobel Prize for Literature (1925) and an Oscar (1938) for his work on the film Pygmalion

All great truths begin as blasphemies.

George Bernard Shaw (1856-1950), Irish Playwright and Critic: Received the Nobel Prize for Literature (1925) and an Oscar (1938) for his work on the film Pygmalion

While we ourselves are the living graves of murdered beasts, how can we expect any ideal conditions on this earth?

George Bernard Shaw (1856-1950), Irish Playwright and Critic: Received the Nobel Prize for Literature (1925) and an Oscar (1938) for his work on the film Pygmalion

The arguments used to justify vivisection are those which could be used to justify any atrocity.

George Bernard Shaw (1856-1950), Irish Playwright and Critic: Received the Nobel Prize for Literature (1925) and an Oscar (1938) for his work on the film Pygmalion

A man of my spiritual intensity does not eat corpses.

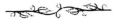

George Bernard Shaw (1856-1950), Irish Playwright and Critic: Received the Nobel Prize for Literature (1925) and an Oscar (1938) for his work on the film Pygmalion

We pray on Sundays that we may have light
To guide our footsteps on the path we tread;
We are sick of war we don't want to fight,
And yet we gorge ourselves upon the dead.

George Bernard Shaw (1856-1950), Irish Playwright and Critic: Received the Nobel Prize for Literature (1925) and an Oscar (1938) for his work on the film Pygmalion

Atrocities are no less atrocities when they occur in laboratories and are called medical research.

George Bernard Shaw (1856-1950), Irish Playwright and Critic: Received the Nobel Prize for Literature (1925) and an Oscar (1938) for his work on the film Pygmalion

Custom will reconcile people to any atrocity; and fashion will drive them to acquire any custom.

George Bernard Shaw (1856-1950), Irish Playwright and Critic: Received the Nobel Prize for Literature (1925) and an Oscar (1938) for his work on the film Pygmalion

> Reasonable people adapt themselves to the world. Unreasonable people attempt to adapt the world to themselves. All progress, therefore, depends on unreasonable people.

George Bernard Shaw (1856-1950), Irish Playwright and Critic: Received the Nobel Prize for Literature (1925) and an Oscar (1938) for his work on the film Pygmalion

> The average age (longevity) of a meat-eater is 63. I am on the verge of 85 and still at work as hard as ever. I have lived quite long enough and am trying to die, but I simply cannot do it. A single beefsteak would finish me, but I cannot bring myself to swallow it. I am oppressed with a dread of living forever. That is the only disadvantage of vegetarianism.

George Bernard Shaw (1856-1950), Irish Playwright and Critic: Received the Nobel Prize for Literature (1925) and an Oscar (1938) for his work on the film Pygmalion

> Animals are my friends...and I don't eat my friends. My will contains directions for my funeral, which will be followed not by mourning coaches, but by herds of oxen, sheep, swine, flocks of poultry, and a small travelling aquarium of live fish, all wearing white scarves in honor of the man who perished rather than eat his fellow creatures.

George Bernard Shaw (1856-1950), Irish Playwright and Critic awarded the Nobel Prize for Literature (1925) and an Oscar (1938) for his work on the film Pygmalion

> When a man wants to murder a tiger, he calls it sport; when a tiger wants to murder him he calls it ferocity.

George Bernard Shaw (1856-1950), Irish Playwright and Critic: Received the Nobel Prize for Literature (1925) and an Oscar (1938) for his work on the film Pygmalion

> Think of the fierce energy concentrated in an acorn! You bury it in the ground and it explodes into an oak! Bury a sheep, and nothing happens but decay.

George Bernard Shaw (1856-1950), Irish Playwright and Critic: Received the Nobel Prize for Literature (1925) and an Oscar (1938) for his work on the film Pygmalion

> Why should you call me to account for eating decently? If I battened on the scorched corpses of animals, you might well ask me why I did that.

Dr Herbert Shelton, American Naturopathic Physician: From Superior Nutrition

> The cannibal goes out and hunts, pursues and kills another man and proceeds to cook and eat him precisely as he would any other game. There is not a single argument nor a single fact that can be offered in favor of flesh eating that cannot be offered with equal strength, in favor of cannibalism.

George Bernard Shaw (1856-1950), Irish Playwright and Critic: Received the Nobel Prize for Literature (1925) and an Oscar (1938) for his work on the filmPygmalion: Song of Peace

We are living graves of murdered beasts,
Slaughtered to satisfy our appetites,
We never pause to wonder at our feasts,
If animals, like men, can possibly have rights.
We pray on Sundays that we may have light,
To guide our footsteps on the paths we tread.
We're sick of war we do not want to fight,
The thought of it now fills our hears with dread
And yet we gorge ourselves upon the dead.
Like carrion crows, we live and feed on meat,
Regardless of the suffering and pain
We cause by doing so. If thus we treat
Defenseless animals for sport or gain,
How can we hope in this world hope to attain?
The Peace we say we are so anxious for?
We pray for it, o'er hecatombs of slain,
To God, while outraging the moral law,
Thus cruelty begets its offspring - War.

Herbert M. Shelton (1895–1985), Father of Modern Natural Hygiene

Tenderness and mercy and gentility, and all the spiritual qualities that set man off so greatly from beasts of prey, are lacking in the lion, tiger, wolf and other carnivores. The claim that man has evolved to such a high mental plane and spiritual plane that he must have meat is exactly the opposite of the facts. He must crush and harden his higher nature in order to hunt and fish and prey.

Percy Bysshe Shelley (1792-1822), British Poet

It is only by softening and disguising dead flesh by culinary preparation that it is rendered susceptible of mastication or digestion and that the sight of its bloody juices and red horror does not excite intolerable loathing and disgust.
Let the advocate of animal food force himself to a decisive experiment on its fitness and as Plutarch recommends, tear a living lamb with his teeth and plunging his head into its vials, slake his thirst with the steaming blood; when fresh from the deed of horror let him revert to the irresistible instincts of nature that would rise in judgment against it, and say, "Nature formed me for such work as this." Then and then only, would he be consistent.

Percy Bysshe Shelley (1792-1822), British Poet

It were much better that a sentient being should never have existed, that it should have existed only to endure unmitigated misery...I wish no living thing to suffer pain.

Reverend Carl A Skriver

The true God is love, goodness, and mercy - not sacrifice, cruelty, killing, and murder...We shall not kill or sacrifice other creatures for him; we shall only sacrifice ourselves for our human and animal brothers.

Isaac Bashevis Singer (1904-1991), Nobel Laureate of Literature, 1978 : Quoted in: You Said a Mouthful, Edited by Ronald D. Fuchs.

I did not become a vegetarian for my health I did it for the health of the chickens.

181

Isaac Bashevis Singer (1904-1991), Nobel Laureate of Literature, 1978

If there would come a voice from God saying, 'I'm against vegetarianism!' I would say, 'Well, I am for it!' This is how strongly I feel in this regard.

Isaac Bashevis Singer (1904-1991), Nobel Laureate of Literature, 1978:Newsweek Interview (October 16, 1978) after winning the Nobel Prize for literature

The same questions are bothering me today as they did fifty years ago. Why is one born? Why does one suffer? In my case, the suffering of animals also makes me very sad. I'm a vegetarian, you know. When I see how little attention people pay to animals, and how easily they make peace with Man being allowed to do with animals whatever he wants because he keeps a knife or a gun, it gives me a feeling of misery and sometimes anger with the Almighty.

I say 'Do you need your glory to be connected with so much suffering of creatures without glory, just innocent creatures who would like to pass a few years in peace?' I feel that animals are as bewildered as we are except that they have no words for it. I would say that all life is asking: 'What am I doing here?'

Isaac Bashevis Singer (1904-1991), Nobel Laureate of Literature, 1978

People often say that humans have always eaten animals, as if this is a justification for continuing the practice. According to this logic, we should not try to prevent people from murdering other people, since this has also been done since the earliest of times.

Isaac Bashevis Singer (1904-1991), Nobel Laureate of Literature, 1978

I think that eating meat or fish is a denial of all ideals, even of all religions. How can we pray to God for mercy if we ourselves have no mercy? How can we speak of right and justice if we take an innocent creature and shed its blood? Every kind of killing seems to me savage and I find no justification for it.

Isaac Bashevis, Singer

Early in my life I came to the conclusion that there was no basic difference between man and animals. If a man has the heart to cut the throat of a chicken or a calf, there's no reason he should not be willing to cut the throat of a man.

Isaac Bashevis Singer (1904-1991), Nobel Laureate of Literature, 1978

The worst sin towards our fellow creatures is not to hate them, but to be indifferent to them; that's the essence of inhumanity.

Isaac Bashevis Singer (1904-1991), Nobel Laureate of Literature, 1978

Early in my life I came to the conclusion that there was no basic difference between man and animals. If a man has the heart to cut the throat of a chicken or a calf, there's no reason he should not be willing to cut the throat of a man.

Isaac Bashevis Singer (1904-1991), Nobel Laureate of Literature, 1978 ~The Letter Writer

In relation to them, all people are Nazis; for the animals it is an eternal Treblinka.

Peter Singer

All the arguments to prove man's superiority cannot shatter this hard fact: in suffering the animals are our equals.

Socrates (469 - 399 BCE), Famous Vegetarian Greek Philosopher first attaining an understanding of compassion.

Socrates (469 - 399 BCE), Famous Vegetarian Greek Philosopher

Let he that would move the world, first move himself.

Socrates (469 - 399 BCE), Famous Vegetarian Greek Philosopher

The shortest and surest way to live with honor in the world is to be in reality what we would appear to be; and if we observe, we shall find that all human virtues increase and strengthen themselves by the practice of them.

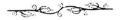

Socrates (469 - 399 BCE), Famous Vegetarian Greek Philosopher

Think not those faithful who praise all thy words and actions; but those who kindly reprove thy faults.

Socrates (469 - 399 BCE), Famous Vegetarian Greek Philosopher

I do nothing but go about persuading you all, old and young alike, not to take thought for your persons or your properties but, and chiefly, to care about the greatest improvement of the soul. I tell you that virtue is not given by money, but that from virtue comes money and every other good of man, public as well as private. This is my teaching, and if this is the doctrine which corrupts the youth, I am a mischievous person.

Socrates (469 - 399 BCE), Famous Vegetarian Greek Philosopher

Thou should eat to live; not live to eat.

Socrates (469 - 399 BCE), Famous Vegetarian Greek Philosopher

The unexamined life is not worth living.

Benjamin Spock

When I was 88 years old, I gave up meat entirely and switched to a plant foods diet following a slight stroke. During the following months, I not only lost 50 pounds, but gained strength in my legs and picked up stamina. Now, at age 93, I'm on the same plant-based diet, and I still don't eat any meat or dairy products. I either swim, walk, or paddle a canoe daily and I feel the best I've felt since my heart problems began.

Joseph Smith: History of the Church of Jesus Christ of Latter-day Saints, 2:71-72, Submitted by Brent Welker 17 April 2001

We crossed the Embarras River and encamped on a small branch of the same about one mile west. In pitching my tent we found three massasaugas or prairie rattlesnakes, which the brethren were about to kill, but I said, 'Let them alone-don't hurt them! How will the serpent ever lose his venom, while the servants of God possess the same disposition and continue to make war upon it?

Men must become harmless, before the brute creation; and when men lose their vicious dispositions and cease to destroy the animal race, the lion and the lamb can dwell together, and the sucking child can play with the serpent in safety.' The brethren took the serpents carefully on sticks and carried them across the creek.

I exhorted the brethren not to kill a serpent, bird, or an animal of any kind during our journey unless it became necessary in order to preserve ourselves from hunger.

St. Basil, (275 AD), Archbishop of Caesarea

The steam of meat darkens the light of the spirit. One can hardly have virtue if one enjoys meat meals and feasts...In the earthly paradise, there was no wine, no one sacrificed animals, and no one ate meat. Wine was only invented after the Deluge...
With simple living, well-being increases in the household, animals are in safety, there is no shedding of blood, nor putting animals to death. The knife of the cook is needless, for the table is spread only with the fruits that nature gives, and with them they are content.

Henry Spira (1927 – 1998), American Animal Rights Advocate

My dream is that people will come to view eating an animal as cannibalism.

St Francis of Assisi (1181-1226)

If you have men who will exclude any of God's creatures from the shelter of compassion and pity, you will have men who will deal likewise with their fellow men.

St. Catherine of Genoa

All goodness is a participation in God and His love for His creatures. God loves irrational creatures and His love provides for them.

St. Basil, (275 AD), Archbishop of Caesarea

Oh God, enlarge within us the sense of fellowship with all living things, our brothers the animals to whom Thou gavest the earth as their home in common with us. We remember with shame that in the past we have exercised the high dominion of man with ruthless cruelty so that the voice of the earth, which should have gone up to Thee in song, has been a groan of travail.

St. Basil, (275 AD), Archbishop of Caesarea

A tree is known by its fruit; a man by his deeds. A good deed is never lost; he who sows courtesy reaps friendship, and he who plants kindness gathers love.

St. Basil, (275 AD), Archbishop of Caesarea

> The earth is the Lord's and the fullness
> Thereof. Oh, God, enlarge within us the
> Sense of fellowship with all living
> Things, our brothers the animals to
> Whom Thou gavest the earth as
> Their home in common with us
> We remember with shame that
> In the past we have exercised the
> High dominion of man with ruthless
> Cruelty so that the voice of the earth
> Which should have gone up to Thee in
> Song, has been a groan of travail.
> May we realize that they live not
> For us alone but for themselves and
> For Thee and that they love the sweetness
> Of life.

St Francis of Assisi (1181-1226), Life by St. Bonaventure: Extract from God'sCovenant with Animals, J.R.Hyland, Lantern Books, 2000, (Pxii)

> Not to hurt our humble brethren is our first duty to them, but to stop there is not enough. We have a higher mission – to be of service to them wherever they require it.

St. Isaac the Syrian, also known as Saint Isaac of Nineveh (Died 700)

> Poor innocent little creatures (to animals bound for slaughter): if you were reasoning beings and could speak you would curse us. For we are the cause of your death, and what have you done to deserve it?

188

St. John of the Cross (1582)

All the creatures - not the higher creatures alone, but also the lower, according to that which each of them has received in itself from God - each one raises its voice in testimony that which God is, each one after its manner exalts God, since it has God in itself.

George Bernard Stanton: 'Bible and Church Degrade Women'

There is nothing more pathetic in all history
Than the helpless resignation of woman to the
Outrages she has been taught to believe
Are ordained by God.

Robert Louis Stevenson (1850-1894), Famous Scottish Author of: Treasure Island and Dr. Jekyll and Mr. Hyde

Nothing more strongly arouses our disgust than cannibalism, yet we make the same impression on Buddhists and vegetarians, for we feed on babies, though not our own.

Robert Louis Stevenson (1850-1894), Scottish Author of: Treasure Island and Dr. Jekyll and Mr. Hyde

We consume the carcasses of creatures of like appetites, passions and organs with our own and fill the slaughterhouses daily with screams of fear and pain.

Robert Louis Stevenson (1850-1894), Scottish Author of: Treasure Island and Dr. Jekyll and Mr. Hyde

You think those dogs will not be in heaven! I tell you they will be there long before any of us.

Jimmy Stewart (1908-1997), American Actor

Animals give me more pleasure through the viewfinder of a camera than they ever did in the crosshairs of a gun sight. And after I've finished 'shooting,' my unharmed victims are still around for others to enjoy. I have developed a deep respect for animals. I consider them fellow living creatures with certain rights that should not be violated any more than those of humans.

Harriet Beecher Stowe

We should remember in our dealings with animals that they are a sacred trust to us from our heavenly father. They are dumb and cannot speak for themselves.

Veda Stram, Vegan/Animal Rights Activist

Spending our energies worrying about how animal abusers are succeeding, wears us out and keeps us from making a difference. And worse than that, it stops us from acknowledging the differences we HAVE made and ARE making.

Publilius (Publius) Syrus: An Assyrian, enslaved in Italy, who became a Latin Writer like his captor who, fascinated by his abilities, liberated him.

From the errors of others a wise man corrects his own.

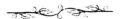

Publilius (Publius) Syrus: An Assyrian, enslaved in Italy, who became a Latin Writer like his captor who, fascinated by his abilities, liberated him.

There are some remedies worse than the disease.

Publilius (Publius) Syrus: An Assyrian, enslaved in Italy, who became a Latin Writer like his captor who, fascinated by his abilities, liberated him.

You should not live one way in private, another in public.

Publilius (Publius) Syrus: An Assyrian, enslaved in Italy, who became a Latin Writer like his captor who, fascinated by his abilities, liberated him.

Every day should be passed as if it were to be our last.

Publilius (Publius) Syrus: An Assyrian, enslaved in Italy, who became a Latin Writer like his captor who, fascinated by his abilities, liberated him.

I have often regretted my speech, never my silence.

Publilius (Publius) Syrus: An Assyrian, enslaved in Italy, who became a Latin Writer like his captor who, fascinated by his abilities, liberated him.

It is no profit to have learned well, if you neglect to do well.

Publilius (Publius) Syrus: An Assyrian, enslaved in Italy, who became a Latin Writer like his captor who, fascinated by his abilities, liberated him.

A rolling stone gathers no moss.

Publilius (Publius) Syrus: An Assyrian, enslaved in Italy, who became a Latin Writer like his captor who, fascinated by his abilities, liberated him.

It is better to learn late than never.

T'ai-shang Kan-ying P'ien, a Confucian-Taoist Treatise attributed to Ko Hung

Respect the old and cherish the young. Even insects, grass and trees you must not hurt.

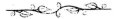

Theophilus (A.D. 150), Bishop of Antioch

When man diverted from the path [of goodness] the animals followed him...If man now would rise to his original nature and would not do evil any longer, then the animals too would return to their original gentle nature.

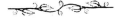

Thich Nhat Hanh: Plum Village Meditation Practice Center

By eating meat we share the responsibility of climate change, the destruction of our forests, and the poisoning of our air and water. The simple act of becoming a vegan will make a difference in the health of our planet.

Henry David Thoreau (1817-1862), American Author, Poet and Philosopher

Every man who has ever been earnest to preserve his higher or poetic faculties in the best condition has been particularly inclined to abstain from animal food.

Henry David Thoreau (1817-1862), American Author, Poet and Philosopher

I have no doubt that that it is a part of the destiny of the human race, in its gradual improvement, to leave off eating animals, as surely as the savage tribes have left off eating each other when they came in contact with the more civilized.

Henry David Thoreau (1817-1862), American Author, Poet and Philosopher

He will be regarded as a benefactor of his race who shall teach man to confine himself to a more innocent and wholesome diet.

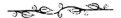

Henry David Thoreau (1817-1862), American Author, Poet andPhilosopher ~ From Walden, his autobiography

There are a thousand hacking at the branches of evil to one who is striking at the roots.

Henry David Thoreau (1817-1862), American Author, Poet and Philosopher

It's not what you look at that matters; it's what you see.

Henry David Thoreau (1817-1862), American Author, Poet and Philosopher

One farmer says to me, 'You cannot live on vegetable food solely, for it furnishes nothing to make the bones with;' and so he religiously devotes a part of his day to supplying himself with the raw material of bones; walking all the while he talks behind his oxen, which, with VEGETABLE-MADE-BONES, jerk him and his lumbering plow along in spite of every obstacle.

Henry David Thoreau (1817-1862), American Author, Poet and Philosopher

Our lives are frittered away by detail…simplify, simplify.

Henry David Thoreau (1817-1862), American Author, Poet and Philosopher

If a man walks in the woods for love of them half of each day, he is in danger of being regarded as a loafer. But if he spends his days as a speculator, shearing off those woods and making the earth bald before her time, he is deemed an industrious and enterprising citizen.

Henry David Thoreau (1817-1862), American Author, Poet and Philosopher

It takes two to speak the truth: one to speak, and another to hear.

Count Leo Tolstoy, (1828-1920), Russian Novelist and Social Theorist

If a man earnestly seeks a righteous life, his first act of abstinence is from animal food.

Count Leo Tolstoy, (1828-1920), Russian Novelist and Social Theorist

A man can live and be healthy without killing animals for food; therefore, if he eats meat, he participates in taking animal life merely for the sake of his appetite. And to act so is immoral.

Count Leo Tolstoy, (1828-1920), Russian Novelist and Social Theorist

Vegetarianism serves as a criterion by which we know that the pursuit of moral perfection on the part of man is genuine and sincere.

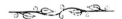

Count Leo Tolstoy, (1828-1920), Russian Novelist and Social Theorist

This is dreadful! ...that man suppresses in himself, unnecessarily, the highest spiritual capacity - that of sympathy and pity towards living creatures like himself - and by violating his own feelings becomes cruel. And how deeply seated in the human heart is the injunction not to take life!

Count Leo Tolstoy, (1828-1920), Russian Novelist and Social Theorist

Flesh eating is simply immoral, as it involves the performance of an act which is contrary to moral feeling: killing. By killing, man suppresses in himself, unnecessarily, the highest spiritual capacity, that of sympathy and pity towards living creatures like himself and by violating his own feelings becomes cruel.

Count Leo Tolstoy, (1828-1920), Russian Novelist and Social Theorist

'Thou shalt not kill' does not apply to murder of one's own kind only, but to all living beings; and this Commandment was inscribed in the human breast long before it was proclaimed from Sinai.

Count Leo Tolstoy, (1828-1920), Russian Novelist and Social Theorist

A human can be healthy without killing animals for food. Therefore if he eats meat he participates in taking animal life merely for the sake of his appetite.

Count Leo Tolstoy, (1828-1920), Russian Novelist and Social Theorist

Man by violating his own feelings becomes cruel. And how deeply seated in the human heart is the injunction not to take life.

Count Leo Tolstoy, (1828-1920), Russian Novelist and Social Theorist

As long as there are slaughterhouses, there will be battlefields.

Agnes Sligh Turnbull

Dogs' lives are too short. Their only fault, really.

Count Leo Tolstoy, (1828-1920), Russian Novelist and Social Theorist

What I think about vivisection is that if people admit that they have the right to take or endanger the life of living beings for the benefit of many, there will be no limit for their cruelty.

Irving Townsend

We who choose to surround ourselves
With lives even more temporary than our
Own, live within a fragile circle;
Easily and often breached.
Unable to accept its awful gaps,
We would still live no other way.
We cherish memory as the only
Certain immortality, never fully
Understanding the necessary plan.

Canon Eric Turnbull, Worcester Evening News, June 26,th 1972

The time has come when we must act responsibly towards the rights of animals and cease to accept the view that man has authority for exercising an absolute dominion.

Will Tuttle PhD (1953 -), American Author, Speaker, Educator, Pianist and Composer: World Peace Diet

Harboring the idea of owning another living being is in itself an act of violence, and our outer violence toward nonhuman animals, which is so devastating to us all, springs from this idea. The vegan ideal of compassion for all life has as its core this same idea: that we are never owners of others.

We can be their guardians, companions, friends, protectors, admirers, and appreciators, and this blesses us far more than we might think. The move from 'owner' to 'guardian' frees both the 'owners' and the 'owned,' and establishes the foundation for peace, freedom, and justice.

We are all harmed by the culturally mandated ownership mentality that reduces beings to mere commodities, whether for food, clothing, entertainment, or the myriad of other uses. It is long past time for us to awaken from the cultural trance of owning our fellow beings, and instead see ourselves as their guardians.

This is the very essence of compassion, sanity, and healthy relationships with nonhuman animals and with each other. I am grateful for and support IDA's Guardian Campaign as an essential step in our individual and collective evolution to a brighter tomorrow for our children, and for the children of all our fellow beings.

Will Tuttle PhD (1953 -), American Author, Speaker, Educator, Pianist and Composer: World Peace Diet

Compassion is ethical intelligence: it is the capacity to make connections and the consequent urge to act to relieve the suffering of others.

Mark Twain (Samuel Clemens) (1831-1910), American Author, Humorist and Philosopher

If man could be crossed with the cat, it would improve man but deteriorate the cat.

Will Tuttle PhD (1953 -), American Author, Speaker, Educator, Pianist and Composer

Eating food is a lot like sex in that the inner images and attitudes we have are more important to our enjoyment than the physical or objective reality of which or of whom we partake. Our taste is determined, ultimately, by our mind.

Will Tuttle PhD (1953 -), American Author, Speaker, Educator, Pianist and Composer: World Peace Diet

Many spiritual teachers have pointed out that when we harm others, we harm ourselves even more severely. The hard-heartedness of the killer and exploiter is in itself a terrible punishment because it is a loss of sensitivity to the beauty and sacredness of life. That loss may go unrecognized, but the life itself, armored, violent, and competitive, is lived as a struggle of separateness and underlying fear, and its relations with others are poisoned.

Will Tuttle PhD (1953 -), American Author, Speaker, Educator, Pianist and Composer: World Peace Diet

> The pollution of our shared consciousness-field by the dark agonies endured by billions of animals killed for food is an unrecognized fact that impedes our social progress and contributes gigantically to human violence and the warfare that is constantly erupting around the world.

Mark Twain (Samuel Clemens) (1831-1910), American Author, Humorist and Philosopher

> Heaven is by favor; if it were by merit your dog would go in and you would stay out. Of all the creatures ever made [the human animal] is the most detestable. Of the entire brood, he is the only one... that possesses malice. He is the only creature that inflicts pain for sport, knowing it to be pain!

Mark Twain (Samuel Clemens) (1831-1910), American Author, Humorist and Philosopher: Extract from his Letter to the London Anti-Vivisection Society, UK., May 26, 1899

> I believe I am not interested to know whether Vivisection produces results that are profitable to the human race or doesn't. To know that the results are profitable to the race would not remove my hostility to it.

> The pain which it inflicts upon unconsenting animals is the basis of my enmity towards it, and it is to me sufficient justification of the enmity without looking further. It is so distinctly a matter of feeling with me, and is so strong and so deeply-rooted in my make and constitution, that I am sure I could even see a vivisector vivisected with anything more than a sort of qualified satisfaction. I do not say I should not go and look on; I only mean that I should almost surely fail to get out of it the degree of contentment which it ought, of course, to be expected to furnish!

Mark Twain (Samuel Clemens) (1831-1910), American Author, Humorist and Philosopher

It is curious that physical courage should be so common in the world and moral courage so rare.

Mark Twain (Samuel Clemens) (1831-1910), American Author, Humorist and Philosopher

A lie goes half way around the world before truth puts on its boots.

Mark Twain (Samuel Clemens) (1831-1910), American Author, Humorist and Philosopher

It is just like man's vanity and impertinence to call an animal dumb because it is dumb to his dull perceptions. Heaven is by favor; if it were by merit your dog would go in and you would stay out. Of all the creatures ever made he [the human animal] is the most detestable. Of the entire brood, he is the only one...that possesses malice. He is the only creature that inflicts pain for sport, knowing it to be pain. The fact that man knows right from wrong proves his intellectual superiority to the other creatures; but the fact that he can do wrong proves his moral inferiority to any creature that cannot.

Mark Twain (Samuel Clemens) (1831 - 1910), American Author, Humorist and Philosopher ~ Letter to W.D. Howells, 2 April 1899

The dog is a gentleman; I hope to go to his heaven, not Man's.

Jon Wynne Tyson: Extract from The Extended Circle.

> All that we do to other species is spiritual preparation for our interpersonal relationships.

Mary Tyler Moore (Born 1936 in USA), Actress

> Behind every beautiful fur, there is a story. It is a bloody, barbaric story.

Vincent Van Gogh ~ Extract of a Letter to his brother, Theodore

Since visiting the abattoirs of Southern France I have stopped eating meat.

Queen Victoria (1819 – 1901), Queen of England

There is, however, another subject on which the Queen feels most strongly, and that is this horrible, brutalizing, un-Christian-like vivisection...It must really not be permitted. It is a disgrace to a civilized country.

G. B. Vivian-Evans, Clergyman

Animals cannot help themselves. They can only hope that someday man will soften his heart and have pity on their suffering.

Francois Voltaire (1694-1778), Famous French Author and Philosopher

> Those who can make you believe absurdities can make you commit atrocities.

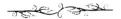

Francois Voltaire (1694-1778), Famous French Author and Philosopher

> How pitiful, and what poverty of mind, [for Descartes and his followers] to have said that the animals are machines deprived of understanding and feeling...has Nature arranged all the springs of feeling in this animal to the end that he might not feel? Has not he nerves that he may be capable of suffering?
>
> People must have renounced, it seems to me, all natural intelligence to dare to advance that animals are but animated machines...
>
> It appears to me, besides, that [such people] can never have observed with attention the character of animals, not to have distinguished among them the different VOICES of need, of suffering, of joy, of pain, of love, of anger, and of all their affections.
>
> It would be very strange that they should express so well what they could not feel...
>
> [Porphyry like myself] regards other animals as our brothers, because they are endowed with life as we are, because they have the same principles of life, the same feelings, the same ideas, memory, industry - as we. [Human] speech alone is wanting to them. If they had it should we dare to kill and eat them? Should we dare to commit these fratricides?

Francois Voltaire (1694-1778), Famous French Author and Philosopher

All sects are different, because they come from men; morality is everywhere the same, because it comes from God.

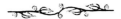

Francois Voltaire (1694-1778), Famous French Author and Philosopher

Every man is guilty of the good he didn't do.

Francois Voltaire (1694-1778), Famous French Author and Philosopher

It is forbidden to kill; therefore all murderers are punished unless they kill in large numbers and to the sound of trumpets.

Francois Voltaire (1694-1778), Famous French Author and Philosopher

It is dangerous to be right when the government is wrong.

Francois Voltaire (1694-1778), Famous French Author and Philosopher

If God did not exist, it would be necessary to invent him.

Francois Voltaire (1694-1778), Famous French Author and Philosopher

Common sense is not so common.

Dave Warwak

We find out where we are when we leave.

Richard Wagner (1813-1883), German Composer, Poet and Essayist

If experiments on animals were abandoned on grounds of compassion, mankind would have made a fundamental advance.

Richard Wagner (1813-1883), German Composer, Poet and Essayist

Plant life instead of animal food is the keystone of regeneration. Jesus used bread instead of flesh and wine in place of blood at the Lord's Supper.

Richard Wagner (1813-1883), German Composer, Poet and Essayist: The Regeneration of Mankind

Human dignity begins to assert itself only at the point where man is distinguishable from the beast by pity for it [animals].

Alice Walker (Born 1944), Author of The Color Purple

The animals of the world exist for their own reasons. They were not made for humans any more than black People were made for whites or women for men.

Alice Walker (Born 1944), Author of The Color Purple

As we talked of freedom and justice one day for all, we sat down to steaks. I am eating misery, I thought, as I took the first bite. And spat it out.

Alice Walker (Born 1944), Author of The Color Purple

I know, in my soul, that to eat a creature who is raised to be eaten and who never has a chance to be a real being is unhealthy. It's like...you're just eating misery. You're eating a bitter life.

Horace Walpole, Earl of Orford, English Statesman and Writer of: The Castle of Otranto and The Mysterious Mother.

The world is a comedy to those who think a tragedy to those who feel.

Dave Warwak

It is right here, right in front of us, everyday. It is like a wavy haze that melts the ground, like a type of fog or smoke that clouds our thoughts. It starts when we are very young and grow, as do we, until it becomes part of us, part of our history, part of our being, what we have become and what we will become.

Dave Warwak

The spirit deep inside us still remembers reality and is unimpressed and dissatisfied with our plastic world more and more.

Dave Warwak

To limit what is possible, is to accept only what is humanly possible.

Dave Warwak

No matter what anyone argues, schools feeding unsuspecting children the corpses of once living beings, and promoting breast milk-complete with its blood, puss, and hormones-stolen from confined, drugged, and tortured creatures as normal and healthy beyond infancy is a socially, mentally, spiritually, and ecologically damaging, unnecessary crime against humanity.

Dave Warwak

Look what we do to loving cows, chickens, pigs, and other
partners on this planet we all have the privilege of sharing.
Humans do not know how to conduct themselves in the universe.
We search in outer space for other life forms; yet, we ignore the
many amazing beings right here on Earth.

Dave Warwak

Hereditary ignorance has become the cruelest and most
destructive machine to ever transpose humanity's destined
natural forward evolution. The scales tipped long ago, and now
the machine has been fine-tuned, magnified, and multiplied.
Never before has man caused so much misery, death and
destruction on such a horrific scale as right here, right now.

Dave Warwak

Instead of teaching our children what to know, let them find
themselves and how to decipher our falsehoods.

Dave Warwak

The majority of people suppress themselves by adopting systems
of thoughts and actions shaped by the perceived desires of those
in control.

Dave Warwak

One must release the past to create the future.

Dave Warwak

We come into this world pure and we unknowingly and with the utmost best of intentions drag each other down from there.

Dave Warwak

Just because we enter into a world with little humanity and know of no other, does not mean we have to accept all we have ever known to be singular, indisputable, and real. The truth is we can make this world better, right here, right now.

Dave Warwak

That which is good and right is based in reality; so too, that which is bad and wrong is based in falsehood.

Dave Warwak

We are lost until we find ourselves.

Dave Warwak

Ignorance, time and time again, imposes its absurdities in complete opposition to reality. This creates paradoxes that one can identify and use to formulate and solve oxymoronic equations. Ignorance fades as its illogicalities are identified and the truth is exposed, enabling change.

Dave Warwak

It took me too long of a time to realize that I am a free, good man, with hands and a brain.

Dave Warwak

To deny our children their freedom is to commit a crime against humanity.

George Washington (1732-1799), Former President of the USA

Labor to keep alive in your breast that little spark of celestial fire called conscience.

George Washington (1732-1799), Former President of the USA

Associate yourself with men of good quality if you esteem your own reputation for 'tis better to be alone than in bad company.

George Washington (1732-1799), Former President of the USA

Be courteous to all, but intimate with few, and let those few be well tried before you give them your confidence. True friendship is a plant of slow growth, and must undergo and withstand the shocks of adversity before it is entitled to the appellation.

George Washington (1732-1799), Former President of the USA

It's wonderful what we can do if we're always doing.

George Washington (1732-1799), Former President of the USA

I hope I shall possess firmness and virtue enough to maintain what I consider the most enviable of all titles, the character of an honest man.

George Washington (1732-1799), Former President of the USA

There is but one straight course, and that is to seek truth and pursue it steadily.

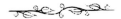

George Washington (1732-1799), Former President of the USA ~ Extract from His letter to his niece Harriet Washington, October 30, 1791

It is better to offer no excuse than a bad one.

Captain Paul Watson, Sea Shepherd Conservation Society

If you want to know where you would have stood on slavery before the Civil War, don't look at where you stand on slavery today. Look at where you stand on animal rights.

Captain Paul Watson, Sea Shepherd Conservation Society

Seafood is simply a socially acceptable form of bush meat.

Captain Paul Watson, Sea Shepherd Conservation Society

We condemn Africans for hunting monkeys and mammalian and bird species from the jungle yet the developed world thinks nothing of hauling in magnificent wild creatures like swordfish, tuna, halibut, shark, and salmon for our meals.

Captain Paul Watson, Sea Shepherd Conservation Society

The fact is that the global slaughter of marine wildlife is simply the largest massacre of wildlife on the planet.

Captain Paul Watson, Sea Shepherd Conservation Society

Feeding fish, whale and seal to children is a form of child abuse.

Edith Wharton

My little dog - a heartbeat at my feet.

Dennis Weaver (1924–2006), American Television Actor, Emmy Award-winner, and Environmental and Animal Activist

There will come a time...when civilized people will look back in horror on our generation and the ones that preceded it: the idea that we should eat other living things running around on four legs, that we should raise them just for the purpose of killing them! The people of the future will say "meat-eaters!" in disgust and regard us in the same way we regard cannibals and cannibalism.

W. Dayton Wedgefarth

I talk to him when I'm lonesome like; and I'm sure he understands.

When he looks at me so attentively and gently licks my hands;

Then he rubs his nose on my tailored clothes, but I never say naught thereat.

For the good Lord knows I can buy more clothes, but never a friend like that.

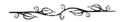

John Wesley

I believe in my heart that faith in Jesus Christ can and will lead us beyond an exclusive concern for the wellbeing of other human beings to a broader concern for the well-being of the birds in our backyards, the fish in our rivers, and every living creature on the face of the earth.

H.G Wells (1866-1946), English Novelist and Historian: Extract from: A Modern Utopia

In all the round world of Utopia there is no meat. There used to be. But now we cannot stand the thought of slaughterhouses. And in a population that is all educated and at about the same level of physical refinement, it is practically impossible to find anyone who will hew a dead ox or pig. We never settled the hygienic aspect of meat-eating at all. This other aspect decided us. I can still remember as a boy the rejoicings over the closing of the last slaughterhouse.

Right Reverend John Chandler White

It is time, fully time, that all Christian people awake to the necessity of taking an active part in the fight against what I dare to call the Crime of Animal Cruelty. Everyone who loves God and animals should help bear the burden of the fight against this insidious evil.

Ellen White (1827-1915), Co-Founder of the Seventh Day Adventists

Animals are often transported long distances and subjected to great suffering in reaching a market. Taken from the green pastures and traveling for weary miles over the hot, dusty roads, or crowded into filthy cars, feverish and exhausted, often for many hours deprived of food and water, the poor creatures are driven to their death, that human beings may feast on the carcasses.

Theodore H. White (1915-1986), American Political Writer

To go against the dominant thinking of your friends, of most of the people you see every day, is perhaps the most difficult act of heroism you can have.

John Greenleaf Whittier (1807-92), Quaker Poet and Abolitionist

The sooner we recognize the fact that the mercy of the Almighty extends to every creature endowed with life, the better it will be for us as men and Christians.

Dennis Wholey

Expecting the world to treat you fairly because you are good is like expecting the bull not to charge because you are a vegetarian.

Ella Wheeler Wilcox, (1850-1919), American Poet and Novelist: Song of Myself

I am the voice of the voiceless.
Through me the dumb shall speak
Til' the deaf world's ear shall be made to hear
The wrongs of the wordless weak.
The same force formed the sparrow
That fashioned man, the king.
The God of the whole gave a spark of soul
To furred and feathered thing;
And I am my brother's keeper,
And I will fight his fight.
And speak the word for beast and bird
Till the world shall set things right.

Walt Whitman (1819–1892), American Poet, Essayist and Journalist

I think I could turn and live with animals,
They are so placid and self-contained,
I stand and look at them long and long.
They do not sweat and whine about their condition,
They do not lie awake in the dark and weep for their sins,
They do not make me sick discussing their duty to God,
Not one is dissatisfied, not one is demented with the mania of owning things,
Not one kneels to another, nor to his kind that lived thousands of years ago,
Not one is respectable or unhappy over the whole earth.
So they show their relations to me and I accept them,
They bring me tokens of myself, they evince them plainly in their possession.
I wonder where they get those tokens,
Did I pass that way huge times ago and negligently drop them?
Myself moving forward then and now and forever,
Gathering and showing more always and with velocity,
Infinite and omnigenous, and the like of these among them,
Not too exclusive toward the reaches of my remembrances,
Picking out here one that I love and now go with him on brotherly terms.
A gigantic beauty of a stallion, fresh and responsive to my caresses,
Head high in the forehead, wide between the ears,
Limbs glossy and supple, tail dusting the ground,
Eyes full of sparkling wickedness, ears finely cut, flexibly moving.
His nostrils dilate as my heels embrace him,
His well-built limbs tremble with pleasure as we race around and return.
I but use you a minute, then I resign you, stallion,
Why do I need your paces when I myself out-gallop them?
Even as I stand or sit passing faster than you.

Ella Wheeler Wilcox, (1850-1919), American Poet and Novelist ~The Worlds & I

Many times I am asked why the suffering of animals should call forth more sympathy from me than the suffering of human beings; why I work in this direction of charitable work more than toward any other. My answer is that because I believe that this work includes all the education and lines of reform which are needed to make a perfect circle of peace and goodwill about the earth....

Walter Willett, M.D. at Brigham, Women's Hospital: Director of a Study which   proved the connexion between eating red meat and colon and other cancers.

If you step back and look at the data, the optimum amount of red meat you eat should be zero.

Ben Williams

There is no psychiatrist in the world like a puppy licking your face.

Woodrow Wilson (1856-1924), Former President of the United States

If you want to make enemies, try to change something.

Woodrow Wilson (1856-1924), Former President of the United States

If a dog will not come to you after having looked you in the face, you should go home and examine your conscience.

Jon Winokur

Both humans and dogs love to play well into adulthood, and individuals from both species occasionally display evidence of having a conscience.

Philip Wollen (1950-), Australian Writer: Founder of The Winsome Constance Kindness Trust~ Dreamers of the Day

In my judgement, the vivisector is to medicine what the pornographer is to art.

Philip Wollen (1950-), Australian Writer: Founder of The Winsome Constance Kindness Trust

Act. Don't react. See a need, fix it first. Worry about the details later. If you wait until you are asked you have just missed a golden opportunity. They are fleeting and rare.

Philip Wollen (1950-), Australian Writer: Founder of The Winsome Constance Kindness Trust

None of us is as smart as all of us. Synergy means 2 plus 2 equals 5.

Philip Wollen (1950-), Australian Writer: Founder of The Winsome Constance Kindness Trust

There is nothing we can't achieve if we don't care who gets the credit for it.

Philip Wollen (1950-), Australian Writer: Founder of The Winsome Constance Kindness Trust

Humankind's greatest sin is anthropocentrism – where human life is valued above all other sentient life. Msirtnecoporhtna – [anthropocentrism written] backwards or forwards it makes no sense. If Moses could spell it, he would have put in his top 10.

Philip Wollen (1950-), Australian Writer: Founder of The Winsome Constance Kindness Trust

In their capacity to feel pain and fear, a pig is a dog is a bear is a boy.

Philip Wollen (1950-), Australian Writer: Founder of The Winsome Constance Kindness Trust

One man [or woman] can make a difference and every man [woman] should try.

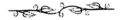

Philip Wollen (1950-), Australian Writer: Founder of The Winsome Constance Kindness Trust

Just because you can do little does not mean you can do nothing.

Philip Wollen (1950-), Australian Writer: Founder of The Winsome Constance Kindness Trust

For the animal kingdom, the Holocaust never ended.

Philip Wollen (1950-), Australian Writer: Founder of The Winsome Constance Kindness Trust

We don't 'own' a 'pet.' We are 'guardians' of 'companion animals.'

Philip Wollen (1950-), Australian Writer: Founder of The Winsome Constance Kindness Trust

A caged bird is proof of the moral bankruptcy of its jailer.

Philip Wollen (1950-), Australian Writer: Founder of The Winsome Constance Kindness Trust

A robin redbreast in a cage puts all heaven in a rage.

Philip Wollen (1950-), Australian Writer: Founder of The Winsome Constance Kindness Trust

Cruelty to an animal is something we learn. Put a child in a room with a toy and a bunny. If she plays with the toy and is cruel to the bunny, I will buy you a new car.

Philip Wollen (1950-), Australian Writer: Founder of The Winsome Constance Kindness Trust

Start now. There is not enough darkness in the world to put out the light of a single candle.

Philip Wollen (1950-), Australian Writer: Founder of The Winsome Constance Kindness Trust

I can understand why some theologians believe animals have no souls. To the tortured animal, the only evidence of the existence of God is the absence of the torturer. In their cages, I would have little difficulty concluding that my jailer was living proof that God is deaf, blind, indifferent or dead. Standing in front of a torture chamber I realised the beast was outside the bars and I was two yards away from becoming an atheist.

Philip Wollen (1950-), Australian Writer: Founder of The Winsome Constance Kindness Trust

The Circus is to Entertainment, what Vivisection is to Science, what Pornography is to Art.

Philip Wollen (1950-), Australian Writer: Founder of The Winsome Constance Kindness Trust

The most disgusting four letter word in the English language is 'CAGE.'

Philip Wollen (1950-), Australian Writer: Founder of The Winsome Constance Kindness Trust

When animals do something noble we say they are behaving 'like humans.' When humans do something disgusting we say they are behaving 'like animals.' Clumsy use of the English language perpetuates the myth that animals are inferior and disposable beings. This makes the task of humanitarians even more difficult.

Philip Wollen (1950-), Australian Writer: Founder of The Winsome Constance Kindness Trust

If an animal ever wrote a bestseller it would still be published under 'Anon.'

Philip Wollen (1950-), Australian Writer: Founder of The Winsome Constance Kindness Trust

Our culture, religion and tradition starts with oral history. Our belief in the superiority of humans is rooted in the darkness and superstition, passed on by word of mouth for centuries. It has become holy writ, large by human hands. If we taped an oral history of the animal kingdom, the anguished screams would drown out the sound and fury of the Big Bang.

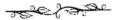

Rev. Francis Wood, The Vegetarian Messenger and Health Review, July 1931, The Journal of the Vegetarian Society

Their life appears just as precious to them as is ours to us...the gift of life carries with it the gift of the right of life, in the sense at least of an equal right to life with all other creatures of the divine power and grace.

John Woolman (1720-1772), Quaker Preacher and Abolitionist who Compassionately Fought Against both Slavery and Cruelty to animals

> Be careful that the love of gain draws us not into any business which may weaken our love of our Heavenly Father, or bring trouble to any of His creatures.

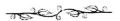

Rev. Francis Wood: Vegetarianism in Relation to the Treatment of Animals, The C.P. Newcombe Memorial Prize-Essay, 1919: Published as a pamphlet by The Vegetarian Society in 1920

> Our opponents...suggest that, in our zeal for the rights of animals we are disposed to forget the rights of men, and are prepared to pursue a policy which would eventuate in the overrunning of the earth by the former to the detriment of the latter. Neither of these charges is true.

> We recognize that the rights of animals, as those of men, are conditioned by the rights of their fellow-beings; that, in this world, all living things should accept such limitations, in respect of their lives and liberties, as are requisite in the interest of all other living things. All that we claim on behalf of the animals is that they shall be dealt with on the same principles of justice which we apply in the case of men, and shall not be subject to greater limitations than strict justice requires.

John Woolman (1720-1772), Quaker Preacher and Abolitionist who Compassionately Fought Against both Slavery and Cruelty to Animals

> Where the love of God is verily perfected and the true spirit of government watchfully attended to, a tenderness toward all creatures made subject to us will be experienced, and a care felt in us that we do not lessen that sweetness of life in the animal creation which the great Creator intends for them.

226

Rev. Basil Wrighton, (unpublished) Letter to a Columnist in The Universe, 19th July, 1982, Reprinted in The Ark, No. 136, August 1982

> Animals obviously do not have human righ
> ts, for their life has a different purpose and function. They would have no use for our social and political rights. But what of those other 'rights' (there is no other word for it) which their Creator must have given them (not against himself but against us) when he placed them on this earth – rights which follow from the physical nature they share with us humans, from the needs and appetites we have in common and our common capacity for pleasure and pain?

John Woolman (1720-1772), Quaker Preacher and Abolitionist who Compassionately Fought Against both Slavery and Cruelty to Animals

> Where the love of God is verily perfected and the true spirit of government watchfully attended to, a tenderness toward all creatures made subject to us will be experienced, and a care felt in us that we do not lessen that sweetness of life in the animal creation which the great Creator intends for them.

Yogashastra (Jain Scripture) (500 BC)

> All living things love their life, desire pleasure and do not like pain; they dislike any injury to themselves; everybody is desirous of life and to every being, his life is very dear.

Yogashastra (Jain Scripture) (500 BC)

> In happiness and suffering, in joy and grief, we should regard all creatures as we regard our own self, and should therefore refrain from inflicting upon others such injury as would appear undesirable to us if inflicted upon ourselves.

Thomas Young, Clergyman: Extract from: An Essay on Humanity to Animals, 1798, (P69)

> I think the English have more of cruelty to animals in their sports in general, than any of their neighbours; which I the more wonder at, because there is no people among whom human life is more sacred, or of more value...

Thomas Young, Clergyman: Extract from: An Essay on Humanity to Animals, 1798, (P134)

Most men, I suppose, esteem it a duty which they owe to God, to beg his blessing upon the food of which, through his bounty, they are about to partake. But how absurdly impious is it to beg his blessing upon a table which is furnished out in part by the abuse of his bounty, and the torture of his creatures! For my own part, I could not join in such a grace, and far from expecting a blessing, should be more apt to dread a curse, upon such a table.

Emile Zola (1840–1902)

The fate of animals is of greater importance to me than the fear of appearing ridiculous; it is indissolubly connected with the fate of men.

Unknown Origins

A man may smile and bid you hail
Yet wish you to the devil;
But when a dog wags his tail,
You know he's on the level.

Unknown Origins

My goal in life is to be as good of a person my dog already thinks I am.

Unknown Origins

A hundred years from now, it will not matter the sort of house I lived in, what my bank account was, or the car I drove....but the world may be different because I was important in the life of the animals and the creatures on this earth.

Unknown Origins

Hate, jealousy and bitterness are like taking poison and hoping the other guy dies.

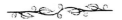

Unknown Origins

Do not repeat anything you will not sign your name to.

Unknown Origins

The dog is the only animal that has seen God.

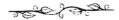

Unknown Origins

Your life may be the only Bible some people read.

Unknown Origins

In some far part of the universe, ten thousand years from this noon, we may all confront creatures more vital than ourselves, more intelligent than ourselves, who will read in our eyes, one hopes, a similar signal. What we want at that moment is recognition. Acceptance. A welcoming into some universal sill. And once in, we would also hope, there is no killing club behind the door.

Unknown Origins

A dog can express more with his tail in seconds than his owner can express with his tongue in hours.

Unknown Origins

One reason a dog can be such a comfort when you're feeling blue is that he doesn't try to find out why.

Unknown Origins

I ask for the privilege of not being born...not to be born until you can assure me of a home and a master to protect me and a right to live as long as I am physically able to enjoy life...not to be born until my body is precious and men have ceased to exploit it because it is cheap and plentiful.

Unknown Origins

Heart attacks...God's revenge for eating his little animal friends.

L et us draw these impassioned sentiments to a close with Plato's ideals: Plato, in his picture of the 'Golden Age Under Saturn,' reckons, among the chief advantages that a man [would have, is] communication with [the animals], of whom, inquiring and informing himself, he knew the true qualities and differences of them all, but which he acquired a very perfect intelligence and prudence, and led his life more happily than we could do. Need we better proof to condemn human imprudence in the concern of [animals]? **(Plato from an Apology of Raymond Sebond)**

Whilst Albert Camus attempts to open our eyes helping us see the world differently: 'Autumn is a second spring when every leaf is a flower.' And asks us to review what is meaningful in our lives: 'But what is happiness except the simple harmony between a man and the life he leads.'

This above record which reanimates the colossal number of 'voices,' proves my belief that: 'all-embracing compassion is wisdom and wisdom is all-encompassing compassion; a universal conclusion.'

As has been shown, innumerable, high-minded, principled, ethical individuals have each arrived at this verdict, righteous men and women from all cultures and all centuries. The hearts of these men and women have bled throughout the millennia, tragically mirrored by the actual blood and guts spilled out through animals' suffering, from a myriad sources. These include hunting, vivisection torture, abuse, neglect, the chain of events associated with the multibillion dollar daily animal slaughter industry and the human animals' callous indifference to the heartless unnecessary consumption of animals.

I am sure that the above compilation is but a mere fragment, by no means the entirety of the world's compassionate pleas for the human animal to act as benevolent, non-violent guardians of our related, fellow, child-like, animal-kind. They beg us to treat these vulnerable, innocent, defenseless animal-souls, with the utmost respect and kindness. Raising awareness of these often lost and forgotten voices has the power to change a person's views on animal flesh eating, which I believe is essential for the peaceful spiritual evolution of the human animal. I wish to end this installment of Animal Souls with the poignant words below.

A hundred years from now, it will not matter the sort of house I lived in, what my bank account was, or the car I drove....but the world may be different because I was important in the life of the animals and the creatures on this earth. **(Unknown Origins – Perhaps from one of the voices recorded in the previous pages)** The compilation on previous pages has recorded for posterity approximately 855 impassioned pleas throughout the ages to present day for the human animal never to harm animals instead to show them the utmost compassion and respect.

I extend my gratitude to the vegetarian author J.R.Hyland, writer of God's Covenant with Animals, Roshi Philip Kapleau, vegetarian author of To Cherish All Life: A Buddhist View of Animal Slaughter and Meat Eating and the websites below.

http://thinkoutsidethepiggybank.typepad.com/so_im_thinking_of_going_v/vegan-quotes.html

http://www.all-creatures.org/quotes/aradvo.html

http://www.veganearthus.org/APE-Connections/index.htm

www.animalliberationfront.com/Saints/Authors/Quotes/

www.kranti.org/damage/spirituality/

http://www.quotegarden.com/dogs.html

Lightning Source UK Ltd.
Milton Keynes UK
UKOW04f1915270614

234186UK00002B/23/P